A MINISTRY OF HOPE

PORTRAIT OF ARTHUR J. MOORE

Roger M. Gramling

Nashville, Tennessee

A MINISTRY OF HOPE
PORTRAIT OF ARTHUR J. MOORE

Unless otherwise identified, all scripture quotations are from the King James Version of the Bible.

First Printing, October, 1979 (5)
Library of Congress Catalog Card Number: 79-67099
ISBN 0-8358-0395-3

Printed in the United States of America

For those who share
a world
vision of the church

CONTENTS

A MINISTRY OF HOPE

Portrait of
Arthur J. Moore

FOREWORD

Roger Gramling has undertaken an awesome task in giving us a portrait of Bishop Arthur J. Moore! How well he has accomplished that task is evident in these pages. When I first read the manuscript a few months ago I put it down feeling that I had just completed another one of those warm, invigorating visits with Bishop Moore.

Bishop Moore's story is not just an account of the life of a man—he was a giant of a man! His story is an account of an era the like of which we shall probably never see again. Arthur James Moore moved in the midst of this era—constantly on the move to stand, to preach, to organize for Christ on the frontiers of the world. Few people in our century have had more of an impact on world Christianity than Bishop Moore. As an evangelist, pastor, bishop, church administrator, world traveler, and in later life a revered elder statesman, he left an indelible imprint on world Methodism.

But, there was more than that! Bishop Moore left a deep and abiding influence on the life and ministry of so many of us who knew him and worked with him. To be around him in an annual conference, in sessions of the Board of Missions, in evangelistic services, in councils of the church, always left you feeling that you had been in the presence of greatness that went far beyond the man to the One who motivated him and moved him in constant dedicated service. This presence comes to life again in the pages that follow.

The church today needs this story of Bishop Arthur J. Moore. Many of us have felt deeply indebted to Roger Gramling for the caring way in which he attended Bishop Moore during his latter years. Roger served him as a secretary, companion, and nurse. Now we are even more deeply indebted to Roger for sharing with all of us, and with so many who never knew this prophet and preacher, this moving portrait of a messenger of hope. If from these pages we can catch something of the vigor and vision of Arthur James Moore, the church is in for some better days ahead.

Edward L. Tullis
One of the Bishops of
The United Methodist Church

PREFACE

I remember the first time I stood before the front door of the two-story, red brick house at 1391 North Decatur Road in the Druid Hills section of Atlanta. I would learn later that the house had been built by the philanthropic Candler family of Atlanta as a residence for Bishop Warren A. Candler, one of the giants of the Methodist Episcopal Church, South. He was also the brother of Asa G. Candler who founded the Coca Cola empire and generous supporter of Methodist institutions and causes. I had walked over from the Emory University campus—a relatively short walk if one does not become lost in the maze of streets which crisscross that area. I had become lost and found myself winded from having made a few wrong turns and forced to backtrack several blocks before finally spotting 1391 North Decatur Road.

Mrs. Helen Stowers, the Director of Student Aid at the Candler School of Theology, sent me to this address to see a retired Methodist Bishop named Arthur J. Moore. She said he was a very prominent and famous bishop. Frankly, to the best of my knowledge I had never heard of him which I easily rationalized later. After all, I was only twelve years old when Arthur J. Moore retired from the active supervision of an episcopal area in 1960. I prided myself on knowing the names of those men who had served our South Carolina Conference in recent years: Costen J. Harrell, Nolan B. Harmon, Paul Hardin, Jr. But, the name "Arthur J. Moore" did not ring any bells!

During the summer of 1971, Bishop Moore mentioned to Dr. James T. Laney, Dean of the School of Theology at Emory University, that he would be interested in hiring a

13

seminary student to help him with some work in his office. Dr. Laney relayed the message to Mrs. Stowers who among many other duties helped students in the seminary locate work. I had written Mrs. Stowers during the summer asking her to keep me in mind for a part-time job. When I appeared at the door of her office that first week of the fall session, she, as if to say, "I have just the thing for you," told me about the work with Bishop Arthur J. Moore.

I had no idea as I pressed the doorbell and was ushered into the spacious living room by Mrs. Blanche Taylor, the Moores' maid and cook for some thirty years, that I was walking into not just a part-time job, but one of the most memorable experiences of my life. I remember that my eyes fell first on the magnificent portrait of Bishop Moore which sits over the mantle facing the front door. To a "country boy" it was the most beautiful portrait I had ever seen. That sight should have told me that this would be no ordinary adventure.

I did not suspect at the time that the stooped, elderly gentleman with slightly ruffled white hair who greeted me and led me up the stairs to the library which served as his study and office would become my friend and mentor. I did not know that in a short time with me as his secretary and companion we would ride the highways and the byways of his native Georgia and that I would be privileged here and there to see a glimpse of the boy from south Georgia who became a giant of his church both at home and around the world. I had no idea of how many people I would meet who would welcome and befriend me because I helped to take care of "the Bishop." And, when they said, "the Bishop," as I soon learned, it was as if Arthur J. Moore was the only one! Nor did I suspect that day that in three short years as time and age exacted their toll and the shadows began to creep in around him that I would ride beside him in an ambulance on his last journey down the hill to Emory University and that I would sit beside his bed as if he were my own father and watch him begin to slip away to that good land about which he had so often preached.

A close friend in those last years, Dr. L. Bevel Jones,

wrote to me after Bishop Moore's death that surely providence brought me to the Bishop's side for those last years. I cannot help but believe it. I shall be eternally grateful for it. I shall be forever thankful for the opportunity which was mine to work for this man and in some very small way to share in the last years of the life and ministry of Bishop Arthur J. Moore. My association with Bishop Moore began in October, 1971, and ended the last of May, 1974. During those years I served as a combination personal secretary, companion, and nurse.

I am writing this short memoir of those years not for any personal commendation. I am neither a journalist, nor a historian. Rather I was privileged to receive some insights and to be a witness to certain events in the life of Bishop Moore which, if recorded now while still reasonably fresh in my memory, may prove of value later to whoever undertakes a definitive biography of Bishop Arthur J. Moore. In these pages I have made every effort to record accurately and thoughtfully the story of the last years of the Bishop's life. I have included wherever possible stories and other material which he shared with me during our association. I have included in Chapter II, which deals with the writing of his autobiography *Bishop To All Peoples*, a brief biographical summary of Bishop Moore's life and career up to 1930. The chapter which follows covers the major events of his active episcopal career from 1930 to 1960. I am deeply indebted to the late Dr. Elmer T. Clark for information from his book *Arthur J. Moore: World Evangelist* which proved extremely helpful in reconstructing the story of Bishop Moore's ministry during the 1930's and 1940's.

I wish to record here my gratitude especially to two persons. I am grateful to my wife, Marilyn, for her help in editing and preparing the final manuscript and for helping me to make time for working on this project. Miss Ethelene Sampley, a former Curator of the Methodist Museum at Epworth-By-The-Sea, is another to whom I am deeply grateful. From the time of Bishop Moore's death in 1974 until the day this manuscript was completed, she has been a source of guidance and encouragement to me in writing this story.

From the beginning she believed that I could and must write it. I am grateful for her confidence and support.

Much of the story concerning Arthur J. Moore's career and ministry has yet to be put in a written record. I hope that these few chapters will fill some of the incomplete pages in that story.

Chapter 1
BEGINNINGS

The first job Bishop Moore assigned me, after I began working for him in early October, 1971, was to assist him in the cataloging and disposition of a collection of files and papers which he had in the library at his residence in Atlanta. It should be noted that his personal library, as well as a large collection of momentos and memorabilia he had accumulated across the many years of his ministry, had already been delivered to the Methodist Museum housed in the Arthur J. Moore Building at Epworth-By-The-Sea. In the early sixties certain other papers were brought to Emory University before the Wesley Memorial Building in which the Bishop's office had been located for many years was demolished.

There were some 225 files in the collection which Bishop Moore and I read through and discussed during the fall months of 1971. They included correspondence and papers largely of an administrative nature from the twenty-year period during which Bishop Moore served as presiding Bishop of the Atlanta Area of the Methodist Church. It was apparent that the disposition of this collection of files had caused Bishop Moore concern. He doubted the historical value of any of the material, and, I believe, there were times when he seriously considered destroying most of the entire collection. Fortunately, he did not.

It would be impossible to describe completely and satisfactorily the contents of that collection of material. It included among other items the manuscript *Immortal Tidings in Mortal Hands.* One file contained several letters from Madame Chiang Kai-shek. Also, there was some treasured correspondence from two dear friends, Homer

17

Rodeheaver and Bishop G. Bromley Oxnam. One set of papers labeled "M. E. Church, South" contained minutes and correspondence of the Executive Committee of the Board of Missions of the Methodist Episcopal Church, South—a valuable and extremely important glimpse into our history. One who loves the Methodist Church as I do could not help but be deeply touched by one set of letters concerning Bishop William T. Watkins and the difficult period of illness which touched his life.

Especially interesting were the files containing material on Poland, Czechoslovakia, Hong Kong, Taiwan, and Korea. Bishop Moore presided over the conferences in those areas beginning in 1934 when he was assigned to the Central Conferences in Europe, Africa, and Asia. It was only natural that after the Second World War, the Methodists in these areas would turn again to him for leadership and counsel. He was respected and trusted by them. The correspondence from these parts of the world reflected certain struggles of the church in the post war era.

The disposition of one file in particular was troublesome to Bishop Moore. It concerned E. H. Rollins and Sons, Inc., an investment house which had administered the stock portfolio of the Board of Missions. An employee of E. H. Rollins and Sons, Inc., had inappropriately managed some of the Board's investments which resulted in a loss of a considerable amount of money. Although the issue was eventually settled to the satisfaction of the investment house and the Board, a settlement in which Bishop Moore played a crucial role, it was in Bishop Moore's thinking a very sad and unfortunate chapter in the history of the Board of Missions and the Methodist Church. He thought that the best thing he could do with the papers from that case was to destroy them. He discussed this with two colleagues in Atlanta, Bishop William R. Cannon and retired Bishop Costen J. Harrell. Both advised him that the Rollins File was too valuable for the history of the church and encouraged him to preserve everything that he had. The Rollins File was preserved, but I doubt Bishop Moore was ever totally convinced that preserving it was the best course of action.

Once the files and papers had been read and organized, the question arose as to where they should be deposited for future research and study. There were two possibilities: Special Collections at the Robert W. Woodruff Library For Advanced Studies, Emory University in Atlanta or the Methodist Museum at Epworth-By-The-Sea, St. Simons Island, Georgia. Some two years passed, however, before Bishop Moore made the decision that this collection of papers and correspondence should be placed in the Methodist Museum at Epworth-By-The-Sea. While I believe that Bishop Moore fully realized the advantage of having this material at the Emory University Library and while he deeply loved and greatly served Emory University, in the last years of his life he came more and more to visualize Epworth-By-The-Sea as a living and lasting memorial to the efforts of his episcopal ministry. He wanted the museum at Epworth-By-The-Sea to be the depository of material concerning his life and his work.

In late October, 1973, Bishop Moore directed me to prepare the collection for delivery to Epworth-By-The-Sea. Accordingly, I boxed and labeled the files and papers for that purpose. Bishop Moore and I personally delivered the files and papers to the Methodist Museum during two trips from Atlanta to Epworth-By-The-Sea; the first delivery was made in November, 1973, and the second delivery was made in February, 1974.

On March 7, 1974, Miss Ethelene Sampley, curator of the Methodist Museum at Epworth-By-The-Sea supplied to us the draft of a statement to be entered in a letter from Bishop Moore to the Methodist Museum stating the fact of the gift of these files and papers and with them the relinquishing of any literary rights to their contents. After discussing the need for such a statement, Bishop Moore instructed me to prepare for his signature a letter that would include the statement supplied by Miss Sampley. A list of those files and papers which we had delivered to the museum was also included with the letter. The following letter was prepared:

April 25, 1974

The Methodist Museum
South Georgia Conference
The United Methodist Church
Epworth-By-The Sea
St. Simons Island, Georgia 31522

My dear Friends:

Since the day in 1909 when I first stood before the bar of the South Georgia Conference seeking admission to the ministry, I have tried to be obedient to the wishes of my church. A number of my friends have indicated to me that I should turn over certain files, correspondence, and papers which I have kept in my home since my retirement in 1960 to an appropriate library or museum. Therefore, after careful consideration, it is my wish to give this collection of papers and correspondence to the Methodist Museum, The South Georgia Conference, at Epworth-By-The-Sea, as an unrestricted gift for the purposes of historical research. In so doing I relinquish any literary rights which I may possess to their contents.

Sincerely,

Arthur J. Moore

Encls.
AJM:rmg

Bishop Moore was never physically able to sign this letter due to the illness which followed a series of strokes on May 2, 1974. He had attended a Board of Trustees meeting at Epworth-By-The-Sea when he became ill. After the Bishops's death in an effort to put into writing his wishes concerning these papers, I swore an affidavit before a Notary Public relative to the disposition of this material outlining Bishop Moore's desire that it become a part of the archives of the Methodist Museum at Epworth-By-The-Sea.

In June, 1972, following the completion of the spring quarter at the Candler School of Theology, I returned to Orangeburg, South Carolina, for several months to work on the staff of Saint Paul's United Methodist Church. It was the only period in our three year association that we were apart for more than a week's time. At that point Bishop Moore did not need me on a full-time basis; his health was still relatively good, and the summer months were not as demanding upon his schedule.

For Bishop Moore the important event of that summer was attending the Southeastern Jurisdictional Conference at Lake Junaluska, North Carolina, which was held July 7-16. In that gathering he was truly at home—senior bishop in the College, indeed, "Dean" of all United Methodist Bishops, sitting on the conference platform of a jurisdiction which encompassed most of the former Methodist Episcopal Church, South. Out of this same jurisdiction he had been elected to the episcopacy some forty-two years earlier. There were delegates to that jurisdictional conference who had not even been born when Arthur J. Moore was elected a bishop. To the degree that any of us know such things, Bishop Moore also knew that it would be his last jurisdictional conference.

Two of his colleagues who had died since the previous jurisdictional conference were memorialized—Bishops Walter C. Gum and Costen J. Harrell. The friendship of Bishop Harrell and Bishop Moore had grown closer and stronger in those years they shared retirement in Atlanta.

Few people could give Bishop Moore instruction. One story of an event which took place shortly before his death tells that Bishop Harrell apparently tried. In his last years Bishop Moore had no business at the wheel of an automobile. (Soon after I came to work for him, we discovered that he had been driving well over a year with an expired driver's license.) On this occasion, however, Bishop Moore was at the wheel, and Bishop Harrell was the advising passenger. One can imagine Briarcliff Road as the scene, and Bishop Moore in command as usual freely using any and all the lanes at his disposal and any curb which happened by. We do not know exactly what transpired. Bishop Moore described it by relating the following: "Harrell acted so strangely this afternoon. Every few feet he was saying, 'Look out for that tree; get over to the right, Arthur; you're

21

in the wrong lane; you're off the road, Arthur.'" By the grace of God both survived that, and who knows, how many other afternoon drives. I have been told that Mrs. Moore often evaluated her husband's driving by saying, "The Lord protects the simple."

Doubtless the death of Bishop Harrell brought closer to heart for Bishop Moore the realization that he, too, was nearing the "end of the way."

Six men were elected to the episcopacy at the 1972 Southeastern Jurisdictional Conference: Carl J. Sanders, Joel B. McDavid, Mack B. Stokes, Edward L. Tullis, Frank L. Robertson, Robert M. Blackburn. Bishop Moore knew each of the six personally; their paths had crossed many times. In fact Bishop Frank L. Robertson, a member of the South Georgia Conference at the time of his election, had had only two bishops in his entire ministerial career—John Owen Smith and Arthur J. Moore. In one of the two hand-written letters which I received from Bishop Moore that summer, he wrote the following the day after he returned home from the jurisdictional conference: "The jurisdictional conference was very good. The new Bishops are all true and proven leaders."

On Friday, July 14, Bishop Moore preached for the conference's morning devotional service. His theme on that occasion was a familiar one in the closing years of his life: "Have You Forgotten?" In those last years Bishop Moore spoke frequently about the sacredness of human memory—that it was a gift from God and intended for a spiritual purpose. "Have You Forgotten?" He would repeat the phrase time and again. In his sermon that morning he spoke of the age in which we live as an "age of doubt." He had seen these "times of doubt" come and go across sixty-two years of his ministry. But, in spite of the doubts of the day, there are some "everlasting certainties," Bishop Moore reminded his congregation—certain "deathless promises," certain "deathless affirmations"—that Christian people must remember and in remembering find new strength. This, according to Bishop Moore was the "religious purpose" of memory, and he hinted at a text from Deuteronomy which was, likewise, a central theme in the last years of his preaching: "Thou shalt remember *all the way* which the Lord thy God led thee" (Deuteronomy 8:2).

Among those certain deathless affirmations Bishop Moore turned first to what he described as the "adequacy of Christ." What does the church think of Him? In the answer to that question lies the source of the church's real power.

> I remind you that historic and supernatural Christianity rises or falls with what we believe about Christ. When we contend for the deity of our Lord, we are not contending for some unimportant outpost or some truth that had pertinence some other day. We are talking about the very citadel of our faith. What think ye of Christ? If Christ was only human, if He was evolution's finest product, if He was the Church's greatest saint, then that's good history. But it will not suffice for these critical and fateful hours. . . . historic and supernatural Christianity rises or falls with the place we give Jesus.[1]

Among the great affirmations which the church must recover, in addition to the centrality and adequacy of Christ and the one which logically follows, is its proclamation of the redeemability and the perfectability of every man and woman under the touch and power of Christ. If the church is to move forward in its mission, then it must move "out of its sanctuaries" in the confident belief that the power of Christ is the answer for the plight of mankind. And in recovering this proclamation, Methodism may rediscover some of those golden experiences which belong to its history. Bishop Moore reminded his congregation that Methodism came into the eighteenth century singing, "not a foot of land do we possess in all this howling wilderness." Methodism came as it were from "across the railroad tracks." It had no cathedrals, and no marble altars. But what it did have was a conviction about the power of Christ—"a power to say to the lame, 'pick up thy bed and walk.' "

Here, as often before in his preaching, Bishop Moore lifted up an element essential to his theology, a statement which in the last years became crucial to his thinking about the future: "No one can believe in the goodness of God and the sovereignty of Christ and not believe in the ultimate supremacy of righteousness." He had grown up in a period of pessimism. His early friends had been devout but discouraged about the future; everything was bad and was not going to get any better. Bishop Moore frequently related how for years he had believed and preached this. And then, one day he was preaching and a sentence came to him which had never come before: "No one can believe in the goodness of God and the sovereignty of Christ and not believe in the ultimate supremacy of righteousness." He threw away his pessimism that day. Christ is the deathless leader of His church, and His gospel is as adequate today for a distraught world as when He first preached it to the multitudes. "We are not on our way out; we are on our way in."

Arthur J. Moore was an optimist. He had seen war; he had seen and served the church in the midst of political and social upheaval. He had seen first hand the destruction, the pain, the disillusionment which follows when men have turned from God. But he believed in the adequacy of Christ for the inadequacy of man. And, as he expressed it that day before the jurisdictional conference, he wanted to "go out" on a "note of triumph."

> I wanted to come here and give one more blast on this bugle of faith and tell you that no cause is forlorn with Christ at its head. This Bible closes, not with the church defeated, not with the people of God surrounded like a lost battalion sending up their signals of distress . . . the last picture is that of a "multitude no man could number," dressed in white, with harps in their hands and crowns upon their heads . . . .
>
> My prayer for you who compose the membership of this dear church, now and in the years to come, is that you may keep the banners of your faith flying so high that others may be made brave and come to stand at your side. To do this you must bend your strength to the cultivation of the deep places of the soul. You must practice Christianity so effectively and so redemptively in contact with the agony of our time, that men cannot but say in their hearts, "Here is hope, and here is salvation."[2]

Several months later, I listened as Bishop Moore reflected on the occasion of preaching that sermon before the Southeastern Jurisdictional Conference. He thought the delegates liked it; they ordered it printed in *The Advocate*. And then, after a brief pause, he rested his head back on the pillow of his chair and said, "I think it was one of the best things I have ever said."

Chapter 2
A BIOGRAPHY

The earliest draft of the autobiographical material eventually published under the title *Bishop To All Peoples* began as a series of tape recordings. Bishop Moore dictated rough drafts of the chapters which were transcribed by Mrs. Nancy Minor of St. Simons Island, Georgia. For some time he kept this material in his desk waiting, perhaps, for an appropriate time to do additional work on it. He had mentioned the material several times after I began working for him in the fall of 1971. However, it was not until the spring of 1972, that we began to look critically at this material. A considerable amount of editing was necessary. Certain sections had to be reorganized to keep the continuity of the story. A final draft of the manuscript was prepared during the fall and early winter of 1972.

It was not a definitive autobiography. Bishop Moore realized this. He had no intentions that it should or could be a complete story of his life. It was drawn from memory and recollections, not from extensive research. It was a very personal statement about his life and ministry which he wanted to make, not in any boastful way, but rather out of a spirit of gratitude. He would write in the opening chapter, "I record only the sunny hours." There had been mostly "sunny hours" in his life. He had never known the ministry to be "dull" or unfulfilling. For him there had always been one overriding passion, "proclaiming the marvelous grace and the measureless mercy" of Jesus Christ. The autobiography was an expression of his gratitude to God, to his church, and to a vast company of cherished friends who had been his companions and colleagues across some sixty years.

It is interesting to note that Bishop Moore spent more

time planning the table of contents than he did any other single unit in the autobiography. Numbering of the chapters was not sufficient. He wanted each chapter to have both a title which revealed the main direction its contents would take and a statement for each chapter which spoke to the concerns of that period in his ministry and expressed a word he felt the church needed to hear again. I recall that the wording for several chapter titles was especially difficult to settle upon. The titles of chapters one, two, and thirteen, "Engraven Upon My Heart," "Memories Too Precious To Be Left Behind," and "Pilgrims I Have Met In The Way," were favorite phrases of the Bishop's. The title of chapter nine, "Happy Privileges, Staggering Responsibilities," was difficult to settle upon as was the title for chapter five, "Go West, Young Man." I remember debating with Bishop Moore as to whether "go west, young man" was not too hackneyed an expression. He liked it; I did not. Needless to say, it stayed in! To Bishop Moore the table of contents was an important part of the book. He especially wanted this part of the autobiography to say something. If a potential reader got no further than the table of contents, there would be something there for him to think about.

The title, *Bishop To All Peoples,* was his own. Its inspiration was due, in part, to a statement which had appeared in conjunction with an article in *The Emory Alumnus* magazine several years earlier: "Methodism's Arthur J. Moore has traveled far to serve the meek and the mighty." It was this thought which Bishop Moore wished to communicate to the reading public in choosing a title for his autobiography—that his ministry as a bishop had taken him to the service of many peoples all across the world. His dedication of the book was explicit and all-inclusive: "To my comrades in the Christian crusade around the world." Among Bishop Moore's favorite photographs was one taken by a United States Army photographer at the Choong Hyun Baby Home in Seoul, Korea. In some way he hoped this photograph could be used with the autobiography, for it captured the theme expressed by the title. A dear friend and colleague of Bishop Moore's, Bishop William R. Cannon gladly agreed to write an introduction. With the Foreword signed and dated, January, 1973, the manuscript was reasonably ready to be submitted to Abingdon Press in Nashville, Tennessee.

There was some doubt in Bishop Moore's mind that the manuscript would be accepted for publication. Autobiographies were not as readily published as other forms of religious writings. The potential market for such a story, especially among the Methodists in Georgia, would be, however, a positive factor in the story being published. It was a pleasant surprise when Dr. Emory Stevens Bucke, Book Editor of Abingdon Press, wrote notifying us that the manuscript was accepted and that Abingdon Press would publish *Bishop To All Peoples*. In fact, the book was already in galley proofs, type set, before we had an opportunity to take one last scrutinizing look at the manuscript. However, once the type had been set, each change would add to the cost of the final product. So, we could allow ourselves only a limited number of corrections.

The response to *Bishop To All Peoples* was gratifying. The greatest demand for the book came naturally from Georgia, but there were requests from other parts of the country as well. The story of Bishop Moore's remarkable life and ministry still proved to be a source of interest and amazement in the life of the church.

Arthur J. Moore was born on December 26, 1888, at Argyle, not far from Waycross, in south Georgia. His father, John Spencer Moore, born in 1862, was a railroad section foreman stationed at Argyle. His mother, Emma Victoria Cason, was born in 1869. He was the first of five children, two boys and three girls. His mother gave him the middle name "Jermyn" which he eventually changed to "James." The young family soon moved from Argyle to Brookfield, Georgia, where the Moore children spent most of their childhood. Leila was born in 1891, Addie Lureana (Rena) in 1893, Lonnie Spencer in 1900, and Emma Kathleen in 1903. Of the five children, only one survives—Kathleen, Mrs. W. S. Sellars, a resident of Waycross, Georgia. Bishop Moore's mother died suddenly, at the age of 37, in 1906.

John Spencer Moore's second marriage was to Minnie Harrell. There were two sons—Joseph born in 1908, and Otis Lee born in 1910. Again, John Spencer Moore was widowed. Minnie H. Moore died while the two sons were small. Mr. Moore's third marriage to Mary Ganas came later in life. She survived him by only a few months; John Spencer Moore died in 1939.

Arthur J. Moore was born into a southland which still felt the effects of the War Between the States and its economic upheaval. His grandfather Moore, a member of the 26th Georgia Regiment had lost his life in that war. His parents' home possessed little in the way of material luxury. His parents, both of strong Christian character, were honest hard-working people. In his book *Arthur James Moore: World Evangelist,* Dr. Elmer T. Clark wrote that Arthur J. Moore "sprang from the ranks of the plain people of the South." His family was poor, but his parents provided a spiritually strong homelife and a good, healthy upbringing. Bishop Moore wrote in his autobiography that to him "home was the place where love lived." Reverence for God was a part of his training.

His father was Baptist, and, at the age of nine, Arthur J. Moore made a profession of faith and joined the local Baptist congregation. Several years later, at age fourteen, he and a group of friends attended a dance at which some persons present danced a dance called the "twistification." Although he did not dance, he was summoned by the deacons of the local Baptist Church to answer for the "sin of dancing." Feeling the summons an injustice, he refused to go. Subsequently, his name was removed from the church roll, and, as others like to tell it, he was thus "read out" of the Baptist Church.

He attended the local school about three miles from his home and took advantage of the small amount of educational preparation which it offered. Following his experiences with the local Baptist Church, he came to grow more and more careless about his religious practices. Around the age of 17 or 18 he went to work on the railroad as a flagman. His work took him through Willachoochie,

Georgia, where he renewed an acquaintance with Miss Martha McDonald whom he had first seen some years earlier when they were children. Martha was teaching school at Willachoochie. On April 26, 1906, they were married. Bishop Moore would comment later, "perhaps we were too young, but we didn't know it; we were in love."

If, in the years before his marriage to Martha McDonald, Arthur Moore had grown careless about his religion, Martha had grown all the more zealous. She was from a devout Methodist family and from the strength of her praying alone it was inevitable that Arthur Moore would "get religion." Sixty years later he would write that Martha was "more responsible for anything I have accomplished than any other human factor."[3]

Bishop Moore's conversion has been often over-dramatized. It was not that he was grossly wayward or had fallen to great depths of sinfulness. Martha McDonald would not have married a man such as that. Rather, he had become indifferent, void of any strong religious conviction. He was a good man, but not a strongly committed man. On the evening of April 21, 1909, in the First Methodist Episcopal Church, South in Waycross, Georgia, during a series of evangelistic meetings, Arthur J. Moore surrendered his life, his time and talents to Christ. Martha had led him to this moment. A persuasive preacher, the Reverend Charles M. Dunnaway, convinced him that his life would never be complete and meaningful without Christ. He experienced through a conscious decision a knowledge of the transforming power of Christ. It was a turning point in his life. He realized that he would never find complete happiness in life without an undivided loyalty to a divine Lord, a unique person, Jesus Christ. Later, he would describe it as a "great awakening, spiritually and intellectually." His life immediately became different as he set the aim of his life in service to Christ.

He quickly became involved in the activities of the church. His local pastor, the Reverend J. P. Wardlaw, encouraged him. What Arthur Moore lacked in formal preparation for Christian service he easily made up for by

31

boundless energy and zeal. He began attending Epworth League Conferences and, with the encouragement of the local Methodist Presiding Elder, went on weekends to talk to lay groups. His first formal experience in the pulpit came in St. Mary's, Georgia. The minister there, the Reverend John Wesley Simmons, had fallen ill and young Arthur Moore was asked to go to St. Mary's to help out, at least until the time of the next annual conference. The influence and encouragement of Mr. Simmons led him in the direction of making a decision to seek admission to the annual conference. On October 27, 1909, he was licensed to preach and admitted on trial in the South Georgia Annual Conference.

When his first appointment was read, and as Bishop Moore often related later, "they were read out in those days as if they were marching orders," he found himself assigned to the Townsend and Jones Circuit in the Waycross District. There were six or seven churches on that first circuit. In addition to his pastoral responsibilities, he was also enrolled in the ministerial correspondence courses through Vanderbilt University. One family on the charge, Mr. and Mrs. E. M. Thorpe, provided many of his financial needs. With the additional help of Mrs. Thorpe's father, a new church was built during that first year at Townsend. For the dedication, Bishop Moore invited the presiding bishop, Bishop Henry C. Morrison. In talking about the event many years later, Bishop Moore would say: "I was such a tenderfoot. I had absolutely no idea about the protocol of inviting a bishop. I did not bother to clear it with anyone. I just sat down and wrote him a letter and asked him to come. The surprising thing is that he did."

At the end of that first year, Mr. and Mrs. Thorpe encouraged their young preacher to pursue some formal education at Emory College at Oxford, Georgia. They contributed three hundred dollars towards the expenses of the first year. So in 1910, Arthur and Martha Moore and their two small sons, Harry and Wardlaw, moved to Oxford, Georgia, where Arthur Moore was enrolled as a special student in Emory College. He took good advantage of the courses offered there, worked hard, and came under the influence of inspiring teachers who planted deep within him a fertile love of learning and a realization of the importance of reading. He continued his preaching in night meetings about the countryside and on weekends, gaining a reputation as an evangelist. However, financial obligations continued to press upon him. He had owed money before coming to Emory College, and his creditors could not understand why, if he was indeed serious about paying off those debts, he was not working instead of going to school. So, after a year at Emory College, he returned to full-time church work.

In 1911, he was appointed District Evangelist in the Waycross District. The offer had come while he was still a student at Emory. A salary of one thousand dollars and the opportunity to preach on a full-time basis led him to accept the appointment. Among his early partners in evangelistic work was John S. Sharp who handled the music portion of the meetings they led. There were some slow beginnings, but eventually the work grew. He was ordained a deacon in 1912 and advanced to the status of Conference Missionary. He served the Blackshear Circuit during 1913 and 1914 and was ordained an elder in 1914. It was during these years that Arthur Moore had some interest in going as a missionary to Korea. But, he was discouraged by those in authority because of his inadequate preparation. The years 1915 and 1916 found him active again as Conference Missionary. Although he never formally enlisted in military service, he was for two years, 1917-18, attached to army service through the Young Men's Christian Association. His ministry with the YMCA took him to Camp Wheeler near Macon, Georgia, where thirty thousand American servicemen were caught in the flu epidemic that struck all across America during the winter of 1917-18. He preached there to thousands of soldiers and ministered in the base hospital to many men, who were dying from the flu. Here he first met Louie D. Newton, who would rise to prominence as a Baptist preacher and leader, and together they began a friendship which would stretch across fifty-seven years.

In 1919, Arthur J. Moore became a General Evangelist of the Methodist Episcopal Church, South. He did not know it then, but his career was soon to take a sudden and unexpected turn. Sometime during the years from 1912 to 1916, Arthur Moore had been invited to Macon, Georgia, to work in an evangelistic meeting under the leadership of the pastor of the prominent Mulberry Street Church, Dr. William N. Ainsworth. It was out of this meeting that the Cherokee Heights Church in Macon was organized. Ainsworth, impressed with the talent and ability of the young Moore, continued to follow his career. Ainsworth was elected to the episcopacy in 1918. In 1920, Bishop Ainsworth was presiding over the West Texas Conference. He had expressed a desire to see Arthur Moore come to a settled pastorate. In September, 1920, Bishop Ainsworth appointed Arthur J. Moore to the Travis Park Church in San Antonio, Texas, and transferred him from the South Georgia Conference to the West Texas Conference. The move took Moore by surprise. He had led a revival at Travis Park Church earlier and had given them his best. Now he was faced with the responsibility of returning to serve as the pastor.

By the end of October, 1920, the Moore family had moved to San Antonio, Texas. There were four children in the family: William Harry, Wilbur Wardlaw, Alice Evelyn, and Dorothy Emma. While in San Antonio, death claimed the Moores' youngest child, Dorothy Emma. She died in April, 1922, and was buried in San Antonio. A third son, Arthur James, Jr., was born during their stay in San Antonio.

The Moores were to spend what the Bishop later described as "six golden years in San Antonio." The building which housed the Travis Park congregation had become so dilapidated that it was well beyond the state of being repaired. After a year the decision was made to rebuild the structure. The church secured thee use of a large open lot in the heart of the city. In one day, with the help of volunteers, a large wooden tabernacle was raised. Here the congregation of Travis Park worshiped for almost a year while a new building was being erected. From the tabernacle services new members came into the Travis Park congregation. In the six years Arthur Moore served Travis Park, its membership doubled. Further evidence of his ability as a preacher and a pastor was seen in his election to head the clerical delegation of the West Texas Conference to the General Conference of 1926 in Memphis, Tennessee. His election as a General Conference delegate was unusual. He was only thirty-seven years old, a transfer from another conference, and had only five years service in the West Texas Conference. As head of the delegation, he was assigned to the important Committee on Episcopacy. It was his first experience in the General Conference.

In the fall of 1926, Bishop Warren A. Candler appointed Arthur J. Moore to the First Methodist Episcopal Church, South, in Birmingham, Alabama—transferring him to the North Alabama Conference. Dr. George R. Stuart, one of the south's greatest preachers who served First Church, Birmingham, had died while the General Conference was in session. In 1924, while Arthur Moore was serving Travis Park, he had been invited by Dr. Stuart to come to First Church as speaker for a conference being held there. He preached in First Church on a Sunday morning while there. First Church in Birmingham, Alabama, was then the largest church in the Methodist Episcopal Church, South. During his visit in Birmingham, Arthur Moore was told by Dr. Stuart that he would like to be succeeded by him. Dr. Stuart's health was not good, and he realized that his days of preaching would soon be at an end. The pulpit of First Church needed a strong commanding preacher. To Dr. Stuart and others, Arthur J. Moore seemed the logical choice. He was young, and vigorous. He had already established a reputation as an outstanding preacher. His leadership at Travis Park had built the church into one of the strong churches in the southland.

The Moore family moved to Birmingham in November, 1926. One of Bishop Moore's favorite stories about his ministry in Birmingham took place soon after their move. It involved a public referendum on an "open Sabbath." As pastor of the largest church in the city, he was expected to lead the churches in their campaign against businesses being allowed to open and operate on Sundays. He knew that his reputation was on the line. If his side lost, people would say,

"Well, if only Dr. Stuart had been here, we would have won." Fortunately, they won the election which was held on a Saturday. During the night and early morning hours some persons in the opposing camp came to First Methodist Church and spread some foul-smelling material around the windows, doors, and under the steps and entrances to the sanctuary. By the time the sanctuary was opened for the morning service, the odor was terrific. All the doors and windows were opened, but the odor was still very evident when the congregation gathered for worship. As the service opened, the choir stood to sing their first selection. As Bishop Moore recalled, "I will never forget their opening line, 'His love is like a fragrant flower growing sweeter by the hour.' " The congregation could not contain themselves. All of the tension and strain of the previous day's election was forgotten as the entire congregation suddenly burst into laughter.

Arthur Moore's success as a pastor continued throughout his ministry at First Church, Birmingham. In November, 1929, he was elected to head the clerical delegation from the North Alabama Annual Conference to the General Conference meeting in Dallas, Texas, in May, 1930. As head of the clerical delegation, he was again assigned to the important Committee on Episcopacy. The business brought before the Committee on Episcopacy was far from routine. A variety of issues faced the committee arising largely from charges brought against Bishop James Cannon. Delegates to the Conference and especially the members of the Committee on Episcopacy had to face and deal with a complex set of problems.

Among the complaints against Bishop Cannon were those which alleged his involvement in stock market speculations. The Committee on Episcopacy worked for a resolution of the charges. Bishop Cannon, in a letter, confessed before the conference his poor judgment in financial dealings and promised that they would not happen again. It was during this General Conference that Bishop Warren A. Candler is reported to have said that the only stock he had ever owned was "a heifer cow, and she went dry on me." Eventually

Bishop Cannon won absolution from the General Conference and was re-elected Chairman of the Board of Temperance and Social Service.

Three new bishops were elected at the 1930 General Conference: Arthur J. Moore, Paul B. Kern, and A. Frank Smith. Arthur Moore and Paul Kern led on the first two ballots, and both were elected on the third. Paul Kern had followed Arthur Moore at Travis Park in San Antonio. A. Frank Smith, pastor of First Methodist Church in Houston, Texas, was elected on the ninth ballot. All three were young men in their early forties. All three were elected from the pastorates of large churches. Bishop Moore would later write about his election to the episcopacy: "I was young, evangelistic, and there was a feeling on the part of laymen from all over the church that Methodism needed a rebirth of its evangelical message."[4] Although it is generally agreed that candidates for the episcopacy do not openly campaign for election to the office, it is reported that Bishop Moore solicited support for his election by asking, "Do you vote the way you pray?" If the answer was "Yes," then he would say, "Well, pray for me."

Chapter 3
"JOURNEYING MERCY"

His first assignment as a bishop was to what was then known as the Pacific Coast Area with residence in San Francisco, California. Spread across the far western part of the United States, the Pacific Coast Area encompassed the work of the Methodist Episcopal Church, South, in the states of Arizona, California, Idaho, Montana, Oregon, and Washington. It included four conferences: the Northwest Conference in Oregon, Washington, Montana, and part of Idaho; the Texas-Mexican Conference stretching from the Pecos River in Texas to the Pacific Ocean; the California-Oriental Mission Conference made up of roughly half Japanese and half Korean; and the Pacific Conference in California. The territory was vast. In many areas this was still the frontier. It was truly a *home mission field.* In the entire Pacific Coast Area there were only some two hundred churches with a combined membership in the area of thirty thousand. Support for half of the ministers came from the Board of Missions and Church Extension.

The Moore family moved from Birmingham to San Francisco in July, 1930, and rented temporary housing in nearby Berkeley, California. Construction had begun on the Glide Memorial Church in San Francisco. Mrs. Lizzie H. Glide had given over $750,000 to build the church and was also to endow the Glide Foundation for the support of the church. From the beginning the church was to have a missional outreach. Included in its physical plant were apartments for young women employed in the city. Also, there were to be apartments for the minister appointed to Glide and the resident bishop. Here the Moores came to live.

Problems which confronted the Bishop in the Pacific

Coast Area were many. In the California-Oriental Mission Conference there was much hostility between the Japanese and Koreans. Two districts, two presiding elders, and two district secretaries were necessary; one set for the Koreans, and one set for the Japanese. The enmity between these two peoples had deep roots in the history of Korea. In a few years Bishop Moore would see it in closer detail as he was sent to supervise the work in Korea. The effects of the Depression were felt acutely. Missionary appropriations were down due to loss of income. Many of the churches and ministers in this area depended upon the missionary appropriations for their support. The geographical area covered by the Pacific Coast assignment made travel difficult and close supervision of individual churches impossible. In 1932, following the death of Bishop William B. Beauchamp, the Oklahoma Area was added to Bishop Moore's assignment. This brought two additional annual conferences to his work load. In those days the annual salary paid to a bishop in the Methodist Episcopal Church, South, was six thousand dollars per year. Each bishop had a two thousand dollar expense fund, out of which had to be paid all office and travel expenses including the salary of a secretary. The expense fund was never enough. Subsequently, expenses would have to come out of the bishop's salary. And, with such a vast territory to cover, travel expenses for Bishop Moore were great. Sometime following the addition of Oklahoma to his assignment, the Moores moved their residence to San Antonio, Texas. Needless to say, they were happier there. They knew many people in the city having lived and served there from 1920 to 1926. From a more practical point of view, it located Bishop Moore closer to the geographical center of his work and made travel more economical since almost all meetings of the boards and agencies of the church were held in the East.

In spite of the problems of those first four years in the Pacific Coast Area, there were forward strides. The completion of the Glide Memorial Church in San Francisco was a single accomplishment. By 1934, its membership had increased to over 700. By 1931, the Western Mexican Mission made up of Mexican laborers was formed into an annual conference. The Methodist Hospital in Tucson, Arizona, became self-supporting. In Oklahoma new preaching places were opened, new churches organized, and some four thousand new members added to church rolls in the Oklahoma annual conferences. Bishop Moore would write years later in his autobiography that this time on the frontier area of this country showed him some of the best in American Methodism. Here the church went to the people. The four years which Bishop Moore spent in the Pacific Coast Area were strenuous, the frontier situation demanding, but those years were good preparation for the six years ahead.

The 1934 General Conference convened in Jackson, Mississippi. It was a difficult and discouraging hour in the life of the Methodist Episcopal Church, South. The affects of the Depression were widespread. From 1930 through 1932 total benevolent giving to the church had dropped $1,166,722. In 1929, the churches had paid a little over sixty-seven percent of the apportionments. At the end of 1932, this had decreased to the point that the churches paid only forty percent of the askings. In the area of *missionary maintenance* which in 1930 became the Kingdom Extension Offering, giving decreased from sixty-seven percent of what was needed in 1929 to sixteen percent of the need in 1932. The Episcopal Fund was depleted. In 1933, the bishops received no salary. In lieu of a salary, they borrowed money on personal notes which the General Conference did finally take up and pay in full. Missionaries were being called home due to lack of support. There was a substantial loss of manpower in the College of Bishops. Bishop Beauchamp had died. Bishops Warren A. Candler, Collins Denny, and Horace M. DuBose were retiring from active service. Unable to pay the salaries of those already elected, the General Conference refused to elect any new bishops. The death of Bishop Edwin D. Mouzon in 1937, would leave eleven active bishops to carry the work normally administered by sixteen. Also, as the General Conference convened, there were some of the periodic movements to change the episcopacy. Bishop Moore saw this move as a criticism of the work he and the

41

other bishops were trying to faithfully carry out in the face of overwhelming problems. Bishop Moore would admit later that this was one time of personal depression and discouragement in his episcopal career. For the next quadrennium, he was assigned to all the foreign work of the church except that in Latin America. His area included China, Japan, and Korea in Asia; Belgium, Czechoslovakia, and Poland in Europe; and the Belgian Congo in Africa. This assignment greatly lifted his spirits. Finally, he was to be a genuine missionary. He would write that "it was the greatest thing that ever happened to me."[5] The work to which Bishop Moore was assigned was caught in the midst of impending worldwide crisis. For the next six years, until the doors on the foreign field were shut to the outside world by the eruption of the Second World War, Bishop Arthur J. Moore worked in every way possible to strengthen, advance, maintain, and represent the concerns of the church on these three continents. The world was becoming his parish.

Beginning in the fall of 1934, Bishop Moore began a pattern of travel which he would follow with some exceptions for the next six years. From his home in San Antonio, Texas, he would travel by train to the Pacific Coast and take a ship from there to Shanghai which would be his base from the fall to the early spring and from which he would supervise the work in China. From here he would go to Japan and to Korea as well. By early summer he would be in Europe to preside over the conferences in Czechoslovakia, Belgian, and Poland. From Europe he would travel to the Belgium Congo in Africa. Then, he would return to the United States. Travel from continent to continent was almost exclusively by ship.

In 1935, Bishop Moore made his first report concerning the work on the foreign fields to the Board of Missions of the Methodist Episcopal Church, South. That report was published in booklet form by the Educational and Promotion Department under the title, "Apathy or Advance." In October, 1934, he had participated in the second General Conference of the Korean Methodist Church. Methodist work in Korea had been unified in 1930 with the organization of the Korean Methodist Church which included three annual conferences and one mission conference in Manchuria. There were twenty-six districts, seven hundred and sixty-seven churches, one hundred and eighty-six Korean preachers, and a total membership of 60,789. Methodist work in the fields of education and medicine had been most significant in the life and history of Korea across the last fifty years. In Japan Shinto religion was on the rise. The nationalization of religion was leading to decidedly anti- Christian attitudes. In his report Bishop Moore described China as a nation caught in the midst of many revolutions. Two systems, Christianity and communism, were competing for the "reconstruction of China." Bishop Moore felt that in the New Life Movement under Chiang Kai-shek lay the best hope for the survival and growth of Christianity in China. In reporting on the work in Europe, Bishop Moore stated his conviction that although organized work of the Methodist Episcopal Church, South, on that continent was only fourteen years old, the church had a mission in Europe. The churches there, though young, were strong and dedicated to their survival with or without the help of the church in America.

It was not until 1936, that he was able to make his first visit to the work in the Belgian Congo in Africa. The mission at Wembo-Nyama had been established in 1911 by Bishop Walter R. Lambuth and Dr. John Wesley Gilbert. In 1939, Bishop Moore participated in a belated observance of the twenty-fifth anniversary of the founding of the work in the Congo.

At its 1934 session the General Conference had adopted a resolution directing the College of Bishops to inaugurate a movement leading to the full payment of benevolences and rekindling the missionary support and vitality of the church. Out of this resolution came the plan for the "crusades" of the late thirties and early forties. The idea for a special campaign for the support of missionary and benevolent causes was not new to the church. As early as 1932, a plan had been developed to augment the declining Kingdom Extension Offering and to bolster the benevolent causes of the church. Teams of missionary speakers were to cover states from coast to coast holding several day meetings in the largest cities and receiving collections. Bishop Arthur J. Moore was to be the leading speaker of this campaign. The first series of meetings were held in October and November, 1933, in cities throughout the southwestern United States. The second series of meetings began in January, 1934, at Staunton, Virginia. From Virginia, the team under Bishop Moore's leadership moved through the South; then across Texas, Oklahoma, Arizona; ending at Berkeley, California, in February. Twenty cities were visited in six weeks.

In 1936, while in the Congo, Bishop Moore received word from the College of Bishops that he was to return home to direct another and similar campaign for missionary support and to help clear the mission board of debt. Several early gifts to this campaign came from Methodists in the Orient. Generalissimo and Madame Chiang Kai-shek contributed five thousand dollars. By the fall of 1936, Bishop Moore was in the United States with plans for what would be known as the "Bishops' Crusade." The first phase of the Bishops' Crusade to stimulate missionary giving was planned for early 1937. In January, the program was outlined at a missionary conference in New Orleans. Two teams of bishops were to be sent out. One group under the leadership of Bishops Paul B. Kern and William N. Ainsworth covered twenty cities in the western United States. The other group under the leadership of Bishops Moore, A. Frank Smith, and Edwin D. Mouzon covered twenty-four cities in the southern and eastern United States. Wherever meetings were held, offerings were received. On Friday, April 23, 1937, dinners were held simultaneously in communities across the country. Bishop Moore spoke to the Methodists by a national radio hook-up. In conjunction with the Crusade, a study book entitled *The Sound of Trumpets* was published. Written by Bishop Moore, it was largely the addresses which Bishop Moore had delivered in the first series of the earlier campaign for missionary support in 1933. Over two hundred thousand copies of *The Sound of Trumpets* were distributed. By the end of April, 1937, over four hundred thousand dollars had been contributed for the cause of missions and the payment of the missionary debt. Once again the church could hold its head high in the cause of Christ. Bishop Moore wrote the following about his leadership of the Bishops' Crusade:

> When my little life is done, and my life's work has been evaluated, I think perhaps the leadership of this crusade and what followed in the life of the church will be counted my greatest contribution to the church.[6]

The second phase of the Bishops' Crusade was known as the Aldersgate Commemoration. It was designed to stimulate and renew the spiritual life of the church. It was led by Bishop A. Frank Smith and included a series of rallies across the nation during 1938. One man to whom is due much of the credit for the behind the scenes work of the Bishops' Crusade is Dr. Elmer T. Clark. As Cultivation Secretary of the Board of Missions and Church Extension, he prepared, wrote, and administered much of the program for the crusade.

There were to be three more crusades: the China Rehabilitation Campaign in 1939, the Missionary Advance Program in 1940, and the Crusade for a New World Order in 1944. The China Rehabilitation Campaign was a drive for funds for the work in China which was already suffering from the devastation of war. Beginning in March and ending in April, 1939, meetings were held in twenty-five cities to present the needs of China. Bishop Moore led the speaking tour accompanied by Dr. Y. C. Yang, President of Soochow University; Dr. Z. T. Kaung, later a bishop, pastor of the church in Shanghai and the minister who led Chiang Kai-shek to Christ; and Miss Hsui-li Yui, a youth leader and daughter of a Chinese pastor.

At the 1939 Uniting Conference, Bishop Moore was the author of the resolution from the Council of Bishops which led to the Missionary Advance Program designed to stimulate the missionary and educational interests of the Methodist people. Again teams set out across the country holding meetings in some thirty-two cities. In an effort to strengthen union, bishops from the previously northern branch of the church were on the teams traveling in the South and vice versa.

The last of the "great crusades" took place in 1944. It attempted to lead the American people away from a revival of isolationism which had facilitated events leading to World War II and to encourage support for international cooperation in the post-war world. The movement which bore the name "the Crusade for a New World Order" was highly publicized and won acclaim from many quarters. President Franklin D. Roosevelt wrote a letter in praise of the movement. Bishop G. Bromley Oxnam served as general director with teams from the Council of Bishops leading rallies in seventy-four cities. Bishop Moore authored the study book, *The Prince of Peace in a Post-War World,* of which over three hundred thousand copies were circulated. The period of the crusades did much to lift the morale of the church and deepen the spirituality of the Methodist people. Financially they undergirded the program of the church, and the two campaigns after unification did much to increase and multiply a feeling of unity and cooperation among the three branches of the Methodist Church.

At its meeting in May, 1937, the College of Bishops added to Bishop Moore's assignment the area formerly administered by Bishop Edwin D. Mouzon. Bishop Mouzon had died suddenly several weeks earlier in the midst of the Bishops' Crusade. This additional assignment was comprised of three well-organized and active conferences—the Virginia Annual Conference, the West Virginia Annual Conference, and the Baltimore Annual Conference. While serving in this area, Bishop Moore led a successful financial campaign for Randolph Macon College. Thus, during 1937, Bishop Moore had the responsibility for ten conferences in eight nations spread across four continents.

In October, 1937, in preparation for another trip to the Orient, Bishop Moore secured from the Japanese Embassy in Washington, D.C., a letter of introduction, the translation of which read as follows:

JAPANESE EMBASSY
WASHINGTON

To Whom It May Concern:

This will introduce to you the bearer of this letter, The Reverend Arthur James Moore, Bishop of The Methodist Episcopal Church, South.

He has been paying yearly visits to Japan since 1934 for the purpose of supervising the activities of the Church in Japan and he is going to make another visit to Japan for that purpose this fall.

Any courtesy which you may be good enough to extend to him will be very much appreciated by me.

Yours very sincerely,

Hirosi Saito

Envoy Extraordinary and Plenipotentiary of Japan
to the United States of America

October (sic) 15, 1937[7]

Later, while in Shanghai, it was this letter which gained permission for Bishop Moore to leave the International Settlement and, under Japanese escort, to travel into Japanese occupied territory in China including a visit to Soochow. It was on this trip that Bishop Moore compiled an accurate record of Methodist owned property in China which had been destroyed by the war and for which later the Japanese government did pay some reparations to the church.

In the fall of 1937, the annual conferences across the Methodist Episcopal Church, South, were voting on union of the various Methodist groups. Although not a conspicuous leader of unification being abroad much of the time, Bishop Moore, none the less, was committed to unification and served as a member of the Commission on unification. The Plan of Union was adopted by the 1938 General Conference meeting in Birmingham, Alabama. For the first time since 1930, some new bishops were elected. Bishop Moore, feeling that he could not desert the mission conferences at this critical hour in history, asked to be

47

returned to the work in Europe, Asia, and Africa. (This assignment would be renewed by the Uniting Conference in 1939.) Japan had invaded China. Millions of refugees were streaming into the International Settlement in Shanghai. The churches in Asia, Europe, and Africa were caught in the midst of spreading chaos. In two years the doors to Methodist work in Europe and Asia would be slammed shut; but as long as he could reach the work, Bishop Moore felt a responsibility for the mission conferences abroad. By late summer he was on his way back to China.

In 1938, Bishop Moore received a Certificate of Honor from the Chinese Government for his service in the field of human relief. It was also during 1938 that he was elected to the Presidency of the Board of Missions and Church Extension of the Methodist Episcopal Church, South. The Board of Missions in the southern church, unlike its counterpart in the northern branches of Methodism was a united board. All activities related to mission work at home and abroad including publishing enterprises and educational programs were administered by the one board. As the time for the Uniting Conference in Kansas City approached, many people were acutely interested in the form which the Board of Missions would take in the new church. A committee under the Commission on Unification was appointed to work out a structure for the new Board of Missions to be presented to the Uniting Conference. Bishop Moore was a member of the committee which brought forth a report outlining four different boards of missions and church extension. He did not favor the committee's report and exercising the right of the minority gathered a group of colleagues from the Southern Board at San Benito, Texas. Meeting there, January 15-18, 1939, this group perfected a plan for a united board to be brought as a minority report to the conference in Kansas City. With some changes it was this minority report outlining a unified board which was adopted by the Uniting Conference as the structure for the new Board of Missions. The new board would have sections dealing with cultivation and promotion, women's work, overseas work, and the home field.

Another part of the Plan of Union which was close to Bishop Moore's heart and mind was the jurisdictional system. This system divided the church into five geographical jurisdictions: the Southeastern, South Central, Northeastern, North Central, and Western. Black Methodists were organized in the Central Jurisdiction. Bishop Moore was a firm believer in the philosophy of "unity with variety." There were geographical differences in the climate and emphases of American Methodism. There were different approaches to common concerns. It seemed that the different parts of the country could be more effectively served by a jurisdictional system under one General Conference. In the South, Bishop Moore promoted the organization of the Southeastern Jurisdictional Conference and served for years as chairman of its program board.

In the summer of 1939, Bishop Moore participated with representatives of all Methodist bodies in a meeting in Copenhagen, Denmark. Among Methodists it was an ecumenical gathering and the first "All European Methodist Conference." Bishop Moore delivered both the opening and closing addresses of the conference.

Over a year after the Uniting Conference, newly elected members of the Board of Missions met July 22-25, 1940, in Chicago, Illinois, to organize and elect new officers. Two bishops were nominated for president —Bishops Francis J. McConnell and Arthur J. Moore. Bishop Moore was elected president by a small majority, thus beginning twenty years of service as President of the Board of Missions in the newly formed Methodist Church. In many ways he was to become the new board's chief architect. Also, he was instrumental in forming the new Board of Evangelism and calling Dr. Harry Denman, who would become a legend in his own right, to be its first General Secretary.

In 1940, Arthur J. Moore came to be the resident bishop of the Atlanta Area. The Moore family took up residence in the Druid Hills area of Atlanta near Emory University, later moving to the Candler home on North Decatur Road following the death of Bishop Warren A. Candler. The

49

Atlanta Area was then composed of two annual conferences in Georgia, the North and South Georgia Annual Conferences; one annual conference in Florida; and one mission conference of Latin churches in and around Tampa, Florida. The Latin Mission Conference eventually became a part of the Florida Annual Conference. Bishop Moore would serve the Atlanta Area for twenty years as resident bishop. He was home again serving an area rich in Methodist heritage and traditions. The accomplishments of that period were numerous and varied. "I came home," he wrote, "determined to preserve the memory of those who had gone before and to help, as far as I was able, to write some new chapters in an already glorious history."[8]

He served numerous institutions of higher education as a trustee and led campaigns to raise money for the support of Methodist colleges. Soon after coming to the Atlanta Area, he began twenty years of service as Chairman of the Board of Trustees at the predominantly black Paine College in Augusta, Georgia.

At Wesleyan College in Macon, Georgia, he was elected by the Trustees to serve as "acting" president beginning in August, 1941, in an effort to discharge the college's indebtedness. Dr. Silas N. Johnson was elected to serve as "acting" vice-president. The Wesleyan campus had been moved to a new location outside of the city of Macon. This move resulted in a huge expenditure of funds to build the new campus. Then came the Depression with the result that the college, unable to meet its debt, had its property sold and operated as a separate corporation. In a year-long financial campaign which Bishop Moore and Dr. Johnson led, over one million dollars in unsatisfied bonds were tracked down and redeemed. And, in time, Wesleyan College was restored to its rightful ownership.

Throughout the Georgia Conferences morale was heightened. Youth work flourished. Campaigns for the benefit of pensions were completed, and the annual rate for years of service paid to the retired ministers was raised significantly. Methodist Expansion Day was inaugurated. In 1949, plans were begun for the development of a conference center for the South Georgia Annual Conference on Saint Simons Island.

In January, 1942, Bishop Moore delivered the Jarrell Lectures at Emory University. These addresses were published by Abingdon Press under the title *Central Certainties.* Bishop Moore's colleague and friend, Bishop William N. Ainsworth, wrote the introduction to the book on July 4, 1942, at his home in Macon. The pages of the introduction, written by Bishop Ainsworth, are among the treasured items at the Methodist Museum at Epworth-By-The-Sea. What makes them so valuable is that Bishop Ainsworth wrote them just three days before his death, July 7, 1942.

It was during 1942 that Bishop Moore joined with a group of business and professional leaders to organize the Southern Regional Council, a pioneering body which worked to improve relations between the races. Although a conservative in the field of race relations, Bishop Moore believed it was an area in which the church had to be involved. His service to Paine College and to other predominantly black institutions was based upon a belief that the Negro in the South must have access to adequate educational opportunities without which there could be no lasting betterment for the Negro race.

Beyond Georgia, his work as President of the Board of Missions continued to occupy a large portion of his time. At the first regular meeting of the newly organized Board of Missions in November, 1940, the situation abroad facing the church was critical. In Japan the drive towards militant nationalism had resulted in all churches being brought into one Japanese National Church. Likewise, in Korea, all churches were brought under control of the Japanese. Methodist institutions were closed and almost all missionaries brought home. All foreign support was cut off. In April, 1941, Bishop Moore was able, however, to convene the China Central Conference at which three men were elected bishops, W. Y. Chen, Z. T. Kaung, and Carleton Lacy. As the United States entered World War II, travel to the church abroad was brought to a standstill and official lines of communication with the church in America severed.

In preparation for the 1944 General Conference in Kansas City, Missouri, Bishop Moore was chosen to prepare and deliver the Episcopal Address, a "state of the church" message which generally sets the mood of the church for the next four-year quadrennium analyzing its strengths, evaluating needs before the church, and setting goals. Although members of the Council of Bishops are invited to contribute to its contents, the Episcopal Address is substantially the work of its author.

The Episcopal Address of 1944 contained a realistic assessment of the world situation, stressed the great strengths of the Methodist tradition, and attempted to turn the eyes of the church away from the paths of narrow nationalism and isolationism to a world vision in which the church again triumphantly set out to evangelize on a worldwide scale. In the last three centuries, Bishop Moore wrote, the years 1744, 1844, and 1944 have been significant in the life of the church. In 1744, Wesley called the first Methodist Conference at the Foundry in London. The year 1844 saw the deep division of the Methodist Episcopal Church in America into the nothern and southern branches. This year, 1944, saw the Methodists reunited, meeting again for the first time since the Uniting Conference as one General Conference. Into this union had come the blending of the individual strengths of the three churches, and now in one united front the Methodist church could set about the work of the Kingdom.

The experience upon which the Methodist movement was built was its great strength and its key to the future. What came into the heart of John Wesley on May 24, 1738, was available to every person through faith. It was the experience of God's grace which made the difference in the lives of people in John Wesley's day, which redeemed and transformed society through redeemed and transformed lives. Such power was still available, the message of Methodism still adequate for the needs of the day. Methodism had never been cast in concrete form and hardened into dogma. It had been "fluid," "responsive," Bishop Moore contended, and open to change, able to go wherever and whenever necessary to minister to the needs of people. Its traditions were "to be sought in patterns of action rather than systems of dogma." Its strongest and most vital tradition had always been that of evangelism. Methodism had always been a "missionary movement." From the beginning it had a "world-wide aim." In the Episcopal Address Bishop Moore stated that "the world mission of the church is the one thing that can save it from the corroding influences of a secular civilization." Though still caught in the midst of war, the church had to look beyond the immediate present to the post-war world. The church had to plan its redemptive strategy now.

> We have developed a missionary program of vast proportions. Our work has been so well established and our strategy has been so sound that Methodism is basically intact and operative everywhere, even in lands overrun by the enemy and from which all our missionaries have been evacuated. Not only must we strengthen and enlarge our present work, but with faith we must face the twofold problem of the post-war world. The problem of relief and reconstruction of our work at home and abroad must inevitably be linked with the task of impassioning our Church for an aggressive movement for the christianization of the world.[9]

The church must continue to speak to issues of Christian conscience. The social implications of the Gospels have been, since the beginning, an integral part of the Methodist emphasis. John Wesley struck a "balance between personal salvation and social action." To the historic concerns of liquor, labor and management, race, and war, must be added another immediate concern, namely that of better international relations between nations in an effort to prevent further war.

> The tragic fact that twice within the short space of a quarter of a century the entire world has been plunged into war is sufficient evidence that the whole system of international relations must be reorganized. The idea that every sovereign state is the sole judge of its own rights and owes no allegiance to any common moral ideal is incompatible with secure and lasting peace. Such so-called freedom leaves any nation free to wage offensive wars

as legitimate national policy. That liberty inevitably leads to crimes against humanity such as the stealing of Manchuria by Japan, the rape of Ethiopia by Italy and the slaughter of France, Poland and other helpless nations at the hands of Germany. As long as the philosophy of narrow nationalism lives, we shall have international chaos because it leaves each nation free to seek its own selfish designs in entire disregard of the welfare of other nations.[10]

In addressing itself to the post-war world, the church must reassert the priority of a "wise and winsome" evangelism. The "evangelistic mood" has always been the "normal mood" of Methodism. The redemption of the social order must begin with the redemption of people.

The urgency of soul which characterized our fathers must possess us. Surely by this time we have discovered that soft sayings about virtue, the evolution of the race and the inherent goodness of mankind will not produce the evangelism the world sorely needs. We must speak again of the ghastly reality of sin, of the atonement of Christ, of justification by faith, of the eternal profit of goodness and of the everlasting loss to those who will not have Christ. We should be particularly careful to deal adequately with the intellectual difficulties and the moral and spiritual problems of the exciting days. Our gospel must be suited to the anguish of our time. But we will not help groping humanity to find the way by underestimating the need of man for redemption or failing to declare that the Cross of Christ with all it typifies is something more than an example of how a good man should bear pain. This generation, like all others, must come to see that sin is the gulf which separates man from God and must learn that Christ by dying on the cross did something for man which he could not do for himself.[11]

The 1944 Episcopal Address was among the finest papers ever written by Bishop Moore. It strengthened his reputation throughout the church as the leading spokesman, not only for the cause of Methodist Missions, but for the cause of Evangelism as well. Portions of the address were published separately by the General Board of Evangelism under the title, "Evangelism As Proclaimed By The Bishops of the Methodist Church." Three phrases from Bishop Moore's address expressed the place of evangelism in the life of the church: "the leading Methodist tradition," "the normal mood of Methodism," and "the gateway to a greater age and a more Christ-like world."

With the end of World War II in 1945, the doors were opened again to the work of the church abroad. Beginning in 1946, Bishop Moore was sent by the Council of Bishops on numerous emergency missions to the conferences abroad to help reorganize the churches scattered and disoriented by the war. The first such emergency mission was to Korea where he spent six weeks during 1946 as a "fraternal messenger" to the Korean Methodist Church. His trip there was aboard a United States Army troop ship and required seventeen days to cross the Pacific. In Korea he found great confusion. During the war the Japanese had virtually taken over the church in Korea forcing a union of all Christian Protestant bodies and appointing the leadership which naturally would be pro-Japanese. Korea had been divided at the 38th Parallel between Russian and American forces. It was obvious that the three conferences would have to be reorganized among the pastors in the South and those who were refugees from the northern area of Korea. A general conference was held at Pusan and H. J. Lew elected a bishop. Bishop Moore's report on his mission to Korea was published under the title, "The Church Cradled in Conflict," by the Joint Division of Education and Cultivation of the Board of Missions. There were to be other emergency missions: Europe in 1948 (Bishop Moore was a fraternal delegate to the Central Conference in Frankfurt, Germany, at which Bishop J. W. E. Sommer was reelected for a life term.); the Orient, Malaya, Borneo, and Burma in 1949-50; Korea, again, in 1951, and Germany in 1953.

In 1948, Bishop Moore was relieved of responsibilities for the Florida Annual Conference as it was made into a separate area. In 1950, he was invited to address the World Methodist Conference in Oxford, England, on the characteristics of American Methodism. In that address he outlined the following as American Methodism's strongest characteristics: an insistence upon a transforming experience of redeeming grace received by faith, a "wise and winsome" evangelism, the conviction that learning and piety go together, the application of Christian principles to social conditions, and the amazing power of adapting to new conditions and needs.[12]

From 1951 to 1952 he served as President of the Council of Bishops. At the 1952 General Conference of the Methodist Church, Bishop Moore was awarded the Korea National Medal of Honor in recognition of his service to the people of Korea. It was the Korean government's highest civilian award. Bishop Moore was nominated to be its recipient by President Syngman Rhee.

In 1952, in addition to his work in the Atlanta Area, Bishop Moore was assigned to the Geneva Area which included North Africa, Bulgaria, Czechoslovakia, Hungary, Poland, Yugoslavia, Austria, and Spain. His mission was to revive Methodism crippled by the effects of the war and to reorganize the work in these areas. He served the Geneva Area for some two years. In 1954, at a session of the Central Conference held in Brussels, Belgium, Ferdinand Sigg, a Swiss pastor, was elected and consecrated as Bishop of the Geneva Area. The nine small conferences, with the addition of Switzerland, were there formed into the one Central Conference.

During this period Bishop Moore was invited to deliver the Fondren Lectures at Southern Methodist University. These addresses were published in 1953 by Abingdon Press under the title, *Immortal Tidings in Mortal Hands.*

It was also during this period of the early 1950's that Bishop Moore had his closest call with tragedy. On a commercial flight from Colorado Springs to Dallas, the plane in which he was a passenger developed a fire in one engine. The pilot immediately took the plane down for an emergency landing. In a wide, open spot of Kansas farmland, the craft was finally brought to a stop. Evacuating the plane, the passengers ran as fast as they could away from the burning craft, soon to see it explode into a fiery mass of wreckage behind them. It was a total loss. Fortunately, all passengers and crew survived the episode. Later, it was interesting to read the correspondence between Bishop Moore and the airline. Bishop Moore lost several suitcases of valuable clothing and other articles in the fire. Although he valued his loss over five hundred dollars, the airline regulations allowed only one hundred and twenty-five dollars. Although a man of great persuasive powers, Bishop Moore was unable to move the airline to "see things his way." It interested me that here was a group of passengers who could have been burned to death, and the airline, subsequently, involved in tremendous lawsuits; yet, the airline was unwilling to compensate a survivor for the total loss of his personal effects.

The 1950's continued to be busy years for Bishop Moore. In 1956, he represented the Methodist church at the Centennial of Methodism in India. Beginning in 1958, he was given two additional episcopal assignments by the Council of Bishops. Upon the death of Bishop John W. Branscomb, he was asked to take the Florida Conference again. And, upon the death of Bishop Ralph A. Ward, he was assigned to Taiwan and Hong Kong. He led the campaign to raise funds to build two memorials to the memory of Bishop Ward—the Ward Memorial Church in Hong Kong and the Ward Memorial Chapel at Shoochow University on Taiwan.

As the time for the 1960 General Conference in Denver approached, Bishop Moore was coming to the end of his journeying in the service of the church. Upon his retirement in 1960, he had completed thirty years active service as a bishop. In his active episcopal career he had served thirty different conferences on four continents in addition to a total of twenty-two years as president of boards of missions. He was approaching his seventy-second birthday. However, his work was a long way from being finished.

Chapter 4
"RETIREMENT" YEARS

"Bishop Moore was not a retiring person," an old friend once remarked about the Bishop's long life and many years of fruitful service. No truer statement was ever spoken! Bishop Moore often talked about settling back in a comfortable rocking chair, but he never got around to buying one. There were moments when he seemed perfectly content with retirement, but they were only moments, few and far between. He could reach for a ringing telephone more quickly than any person I have known and get to his desk with the agility of a man one-third his years.

Although he was retired from the active supervision of an episcopal area in 1960, at the age of 71, and consigned to the class of "inactive" or "retired" bishops, retirement was the farthest thing from Arthur J. Moore's mind. The church had been good to him, he often related. He had been an active bishop for thirty years, a tenure most bishops can only dream about. He had served his church to the far corners of the earth often in difficult and even hazardous times. Any other man would have relished retirement and the peace and quiet it would bring, but not Bishop Moore.

He chose to do again what he had done in the early years of his ministry—to be a traveling evangelist, to travel from town to town holding preaching missions and revivals. To support this ministry, a group of his friends in Georgia formed the "Arthur J. Moore Evangelistic Association" which adopted as its motto, "The welfare of our nation and the vitality of our faith are intimately related." Officers of the Arthur J. Moore Evangelistic Association included Mr. William N. Banks, Chairman; Mr. W. O. Duvall, Vice Chairman; Mr. F. M. Bird, Vice Chairman; and Mr. Walter L.

Richard, Secretary-Treasurer. Office space was provided in downtown Atlanta in the Candler Building owned at the time by Emory University. Sufficient capital was raised by the officers of the Association to cover expenses and to provide the Bishop with a salary, a provision which continued into the last years of his life.

Beginning in the early sixties Bishop Moore conducted some two hundred preaching missions across the United States, many in the larger Methodist churches, some in city-wide or area-wide crusades. He was a fulltime evangelist again, and the part suited him. The backing of the Association made it possible for him to accept as many invitations as he felt his physical strength adequate to fulfill. His friends often pleaded with him to slow down, to rest more between preaching engagements, but he seldom took that advice. He was in a real way coming full circle back to the beginnings of his ministry as an evangelist when youth and fervor had combined to mark him as a rising star on the church's horizon. Now age was taking its toll, but the passion for preaching was still alive and strong within his heart.

The period of the 1960's was not, however, without its personal sadness for Bishop Moore. In 1964, Mrs. Moore died after a prolonged and painful illness. Everyone who admired the inner beauty and deep religious faith which was the essence of her life, likewise, stood in awe of the courage and hope with which she faced illness and death. She was a truly remarkable lady. She insisted that the bishop continue his preaching. He had had to be away from home and family so often during his active episcopal career that there were no problems at home which Mrs. Moore could not handle, including her own illness. She had always believed in and stood one hundred percent in support of her husband's ministry. Nothing must interfere with the important work "Papa" had to do.

There was a profound loneliness in his life after her death. In the years that I knew him he did not speak of it very often, but one could sense it. Mrs. Moore was a small woman in physical stature only! She was overwhelming in every other way. So often from the far corners of the world, the bishop had come home to this source of stability, support, and spiritual power. She was a renewing, revitalizing power in the life of her husband. Her death left a vacant place no one else could fill in his life.

Bishop and Mrs. Moore had built a comfortable retirement home at Epworth-By-The-Sea in which to spend some of their last years together. After Mrs. Moore's death, the bishop had planned that the house would go to his son, Harry, himself a Methodist minister, who, in spite of blindness, was serving so capably at Magnolia Manor, a retirement home of the South Georgia Conference in Americus, Georgia. Harry's health had not been good, and Bishop Moore hoped that Harry and his wife, Alice, might enjoy the house in their retirement years. Again, death intervened. Harry died in December, 1969. In time, the bishop sold the home to Epworth-By-The-Sea as a residence for the Superintendent of the Methodist Center.

There were other activities to which the bishop gave his time and talent during the years following his retirement. He continued to serve Emory University in Atlanta. Bishop Moore had come to the Board of Trustees of Emory University in 1943. He served many years as Vice Chairman of the Board. As an emeritus member of the Board, he maintained an active interest in the university's progress and growth, regularly attending the meetings of the Board of Trustees. It is not an overstatement to suggest that Bishop Moore was the key person instrumental in interesting Miss Margaret Pitts and the officers of the Pitts Foundation in funding the remodeling of the theology library building at the university's Candler School of Theology which now bears the name, The Pitts Theology Library.

The Pitts Foundation was organized during the years Bishop Moore served as presiding bishop of the Atlanta Area by Mr. W. I. H. Pitts, a Methodist layman of Waverly Hall, Georgia, and his wife. On one occasion Bishop Moore related to me his first meeting with Mr. Pitts: "This layman came in one day stating that he and his wife would like to do something to help the Methodist church and especially the

Methodist institutions in Georgia. I admired his intentions but doubted that he had the resources to underwrite the kind of program he wanted to organize. You can imagine my surprise when he placed on my desk a substantial portfolio of stock with which to organize a foundation. I was over-whelmed. This is how the Pitts Foundation began."

After the deaths of Mr. and Mrs. Pitts, Bishop Moore continued to guide and advise their daughter, Miss Margaret Pitts, and the other officers of the Foundation's Board in responding to the financial needs of Methodist institutions in Georgia. Among those institutions, Emory University, the Methodist colleges in Georgia, and Epworth-By-The-Sea have been recipients of gifts from the Pitts Foundation. Bishop Moore served as chairman of the Pitts Foundation Board until April 10, 1974, when, realizing the failing state of his health, he chose to step down. Judge Thomas O. Marshall of Americus, Georgia, succeeded him.

If, among all the boards of trust and institutions which Bishop Arthur J. Moore served in his long career, there was a favorite, that surely had to be Epworth-By-The-Sea, the South Georgia Conference Center on St. Simons Island. Epworth-By-The-Sea began in 1950 with the purchase of a parcel of land and several buildings which composed the old Hamilton Plantation. Its first purpose was to serve the growing youth program of the conference as a center for retreats and rallies. The development of Epworth-By-The-Sea began with the visionary leadership of Bishop Moore and the financial backing of a group of dedicated Methodist laymen. Bishop Moore envisioned a center which would be both inspiring in its beauty and useful in its appeal to visiting Christian groups.

Arthur J. Moore had a remarkable talent for raising money. Epworth-By-The-Sea is a monument to his leadership and especially to that talent. The late Julian Strickland, a Valdosta businessman and member of the earliest group of laymen who gave so generously to Epworth-By-The-Sea, once remarked, "Bishop Moore is the best friend I have, but it sure has cost me!" Bishop Moore's appeals for money were always specific. Each project was carefully thought through and planned in advance. There would be a tangible project in which contributors could invest their giving and see the results of their investment. Bishop Moore cultivated continuously a wide circle of friends upon whom he could call for a specific need. He was a visionary fund raiser, but he always took pains to share the vision, often in very personal ways, with others. In that certain winsomeness of his personality he could make others sense deeply that they had a large part in the specific project. His attitude to those who through their gifts had helped to build and develop facilities was always one of abiding gratitude. Bishop Moore never forgot his friends! He corresponded with them regularly. It was not at all unusual for him to dictate on a given day two or three letters to old friends who had been a part of something twenty years earlier and for which he was still most grateful. One never got off of Bishop Moore's "list."

The bishop's "House Party" was one of the ways Bishop Moore expressed his gratitude. Once or twice each year friends who had supported the development of Epworth-By-The-Sea were invited to be guests at the Methodist Center for several days. A special schedule was planned, but generally it was a time to enjoy the beauty and hospitality of Epworth-By-The-Sea. Through the House Party the bishop continued to involve and interest this group of friends in the growth and expansion of the Center. Bishop Moore's last House Party was held in November, 1973. After the bishop's death, Epworth-By-The-Sea continued the custom of holding the House Party annually under the leadership of the Center's Superintendent and Bishop William R. Cannon.

One of the stories which Bishop Moore told in his last years concerned how the money to construct one of the buildings at Epworth-By-The-Sea came as a result of something which happened involving Emory University in Atlanta. The publication of Dr. Thomas J. J. Altizer's book *The Gospel of Christian Atheism* in 1966 and the subsequent revival of the "death of God" theology caused an uproar across the church, especially in the South. Dr.

Altizer was a member of the faculty at Emory University. It was to be expected that a part of the public disfavor with the book's publication came to be directed at Emory University as well as the author. A dedicated Methodist layperson, Mrs. William S. Booth, had planned a substantial gift to Emory University. However, the publication of Altizer's book was a significant factor in causing her to reconsider her plans. Instead, Mrs. Booth directed her gift to Epworth-By-The-Sea—a gift which made possible the construction of an attractive housing unit at the Methodist Center.

Throughout the last years of his life Bishop Moore continued to labor in behalf of Epworth-By-The-Sea. In the three years before his death he saw the completion of the Strickland Annex to the Museum Building given in memory of Mr. Frank Strickland by his family. One of his longtime dreams, the renovation of the old main house from Hamilton Plantation days, was undertaken and completed through the generosity of Mr. and Mrs. J. H. Harvey of Nashville, Georgia. It now is an attractive guest house.

Bishop Moore loved Epworth-By-The-Sea. He visited there frequently. It was a retreat, a place of relaxation. He saw in Epworth-By-The-Sea a link to the past for the "people called Methodist." Nearby was Fort Frederica. Here on this island John and Charles Wesley had landed as young clergymen in the Church of England. He wanted Methodists to know and understand this historical relationship to the Wesleys and to take pride in it. He also wanted Epworth-By-The-Sea to be a place of renewing beauty and inspiration for the spirit. From it one could go out replenished with the values of the faith and made more aware of the goodness and the glory of God.

The Council of Bishops chose Epworth-By-The-Sea as its meeting place prior to the convening of the 1972 General Conference in Atlanta, Georgia, in April. It was a source of great personal pride to the Bishop that his colleagues would come there for the meeting. I suspect that many sensed that their friend, Arthur Moore, would not be among them much longer. Bishop John Owen Smith was the host bishop. I had driven Bishop Moore to St. Simons Island on Friday, April

7, in advance of the meeting of the Council of Bishops, and flew back to Atlanta the following day. I was prepared to return the following week after the Council Meeting to drive Bishop Moore back to Atlanta. He called to say that he had prevailed on Bishop James Armstrong to drive him and the car back to Atlanta. I wish I could have been privileged to hear the conversation of these two men. One cannot picture Arthur J. Moore, senior bishop from the "old school," and James Armstrong, young bishop from a more "contemporary school," driving through south Georgia together without feeling that our United Methodist Church is alive and well—that the past and the future meet and draw strength from each other.

Bishop Moore's continuing service to these boards and institutions of the church was extremely important to him. Advancing age did not deter his commitment. He took personally and conscientiously these positions of service and leadership. Perhaps one could say that he remained too long in certain positions. This is one criticism of his ministry which has some degree of validity. Bishop Moore was not a man to let go, to give up, especially in those places where he had served so well and so long. It was not that he wanted to be a dominating figure but rather that the level of his personal commitment was so deep that he could not give up without exhausting the last remaining bit of energy. He wanted to fulfill his responsibilities to the very last moment of his life. He wanted to prove faithful in all that had been committed to his care. His responsibilities and his obligations were a passion with him. He had always met them. In those last years the responsibilities were not as great nor as many, but fulfilling them was as passionate a cause with him as it had ever been.

Bishop Moore enjoyed the last years of his life. Frequently he joined his friend of many years Dr. Louie D. Newton in attending meetings of the Ten Club, a group of Atlanta professional and business leaders who regularly gathered to socialize, share, and enjoy each other's company. Dr. Newton, a prominent retired Baptist leader, lived nearby and was a regular visitor in Bishop Moore's home.

He enjoyed the many visitors and friends who came by to visit with him. His fellow bishops kept in close touch with him, especially Bishop William R. Cannon and Bishop Earl G. Hunt, Jr. As a seminary student Bishop and Mrs. Hunt had lived in the Moore's garage apartment. Dr. L. Bevel Jones who served nearby at the First United Methodist Church in Decatur, Georgia, was a frequent visitor. There was no friend whom Bishop Moore desired to see more than Bev Jones. Often in those last years the Bishop would join an old friend, Mr. Hugh Howell, Sr., for lunch downtown, usually at Herron's Restaurant. His friends were many. He corresponded with numerous persons whose lives were a part of the history of the church—retired missionaries, bishops, ministers, board executives. He especially wanted to write occasionally to the widows of a number of his episcopal colleagues. To keep in touch with the widows of those men who were his friends and who had faithfully served the church was important to him.

By the early 1970's invitations to preach continued to come, but less frequently. Largely the invitations were for Sunday morning services only. During the last three years of his life, Bishop Moore made one last trip to San Antonio, Texas, to preach at Travis Park United Methodist Church where he had served from 1920 to 1926 and to visit with his daughter, Mrs. Lowell V. Means. There was, likewise, one last trip to Birmingham, Alabama, to take part in a series of services at the First United Methodist Church, in which former ministers were returning to preach. Bishop Moore had served First Church, Birmingham, from 1926 until his election to the episcopacy in 1930. There were a few preaching engagements in Florida during those last years, but mainly the bishop stayed close to home. His strength was failing, and he was not physically able to travel long distances.

On March 26, 1972, he preached in a special service at the United Methodist Church in Argyle, Georgia, which was named in his honor. The brief visit to Argyle was a special time for him. This was the place of his birth, and it held for him memories of his beginnings.

On a similar mission in June of 1973, we drove to Brookfield, Georgia, his boyhood home, where Bishop Moore preached in a special service at the Brookfield United Methodist Church. A plaque was placed in the church that day to commemorate Bishop Moore's association with the Brookfield Church. Members of his family had come to join him for the service at Brookfield that day. Following the service and dinner at the Brookfield United Methodist Church, Bishop Moore gathered with members of the family at the graves of his parents in the cemetery nearby and led in prayer before they departed to go their separate ways home. In the three years I was with Bishop Arthur J. Moore we frequently drove through Brookfield, Georgia. We never passed that way without his wanting to stop for a few minutes to stand at the graves of his parents. Arthur J. Moore traveled a world-wide circuit on behalf of his church. He crossed the ocean some one hundred times in his lifetime; he traveled to the ends of the earth, but he never forgot his beginnings, his roots. He never forgot that the mortal remains of his dear parents lay in a quiet, little cemetery in a small settlement in south Georgia named Brookfield.

It is hard to grow old. It is even harder to grow old and not be appreciated or cared about. Older people need to sense that they are remembered, that there are those who care about them and who are interested in them. Bishop Moore lived his last years in the knowledge of the gratitude and affection of many people. Those last years were not without a full measure of honors and accomplishments. The publication of his autobiography, *Bishop To All Peoples*, was for Bishop Moore a source of pride and accomplishment. That the book was accepted for publication and that sales of the book did so well brought him much satisfaction. It served to convince him that he was not a "has been," that his life and ministry still met with the approval and appreciation of people.

In addition to the publication of the autobiography, there was the production of a thirty minute documentary film on his life. A part of the "Great Georgians Series," the film was produced by the Center for Continuing Education of the

University of Georgia. Mr. Chuck Bowen supervised the direction and production of the film. An old friend of the bishop's, Dr. Norman Vincent Peale, did the narration. Madame Chiang Kai-shek sent a taped statement to be included in the film. Scenes were videotaped in the Bishop's home in Atlanta as well as at St. Simons Island. Prior to its first public broadcast, a private showing of the film was arranged at the Bishop's home. I remember that Bishop Moore was very favorably impressed with the film except for one scene which pictured an old, run-down church structure somewhere in a rural setting. For me it symbolized the small, one-room meeting house of a century ago where Methodism took hold especially across the Southland. It brought back memories. Well, the bishop did not think too much of it. To him it made the church appear desolate and dilapidated and that was not the impression which he wanted the public to have of the church today. Although he raised the objection, he did not insist that the scene be cut from the film. Later his maid Mrs. Taylor remarked to me that the Bishop had just forgotten—that there were a lot of churches which looked just that bad back when the bishop started preaching. The film was first aired publicly on August 6, 1973. Its availability through the Film Library of the Georgia Center for Continuing Education made it possible for local churches to secure the film and use it for small groups and other programs. Many did so.

In the fall of 1973, the new chapel at the First United Methodist Church in Waycross, Georgia, was dedicated in Bishop Moore's honor. Bishop Moore had always felt close to the church in Waycross. At its altar he had made his commitment to Christ and from it he had entered Christian work. He was present earlier when ground was broken for the construction of the new sanctuary and chapel. The altar rail from the old church building where the bishop had knelt as a young man was preserved and placed in the Arthur J. Moore Chapel and a section of it brought to Epworth-By-The-Sea for the Moore Room in the Methodist Museum. The portrait which hangs at the entrance to the Arthur J. Moore

Chapel was a gift from Bishop Moore to the First United Methodist Church.

Bishop Moore received a number of honorary degrees in his lifetime. The last recognition of this nature came from Paine College in Augusta, Georgia. Founded in 1882, Paine College began as a joint educational venture of the Methodist Episcopal Church, South, and the Colored Methodist Episcopal Church. As presiding bishop of the Atlanta Area, Bishop Moore served Paine College as trustee chairman for twenty years. On February 15, 1974, Bishop Moore made his last trip to Paine College. In a Founders' Day Convocation in Gilbert-Lambuth Memorial Chapel, an honorary degree was conferred upon him by Paine College President Dr. Lucius H. Pitts.

In the spring of 1973, Emory University announced the establishment of the Arthur J. Moore Chair of Evangelism in its Candler School of Theology. In an interview which was published in the May 4, 1973, edition of *The Atlanta Consititution*, Bishop Moore is reported as having said, "It beats anything they could have put on my tombstone. I couldn't have enjoyed it after I was dead." The chair was financed largely through the gift of one man, a friend of the bishop's, an outstanding Methodist layman who wished to remain anonymous. Many months earlier several laymen had called on Bishop Moore to discuss with him the idea of a chair for studies in evangelism at the Candler School of Theology. Their idea was that a United Methodist seminary should offer some specific preparation in this field. After meeting with them, Bishop Moore shared with me his feeling that while the idea was very good, raising money for such a cause at that time would be extremely difficult. He said frankly, "I don't think they will be able to get the money for it."

Months passed and little was said about the project. March 31st found us on the road to visit an old friend of the bishop's and a preaching engagement the following day in this friend's home church. As we were seated in our host's den that evening following dinner, he began to share with us some plans he was making as to the disposition of his assets. "My children," he said, "have told me that they have all they will need or want, and they have encouraged me to do with my estate whatever I want to." Shortly, he took from his coat pocket a page on which were listed the causes to which he was giving the bulk of his estate. Among them was "Emory University" for the "Arthur J. Moore Chair of Evangelism." I had not before seen the bishop so taken by surprise. Prior to that moment, I do not believe he had any indication that this friend of so many years was going to endow the Chair of Evangelism and, as we learned later, insist that it bear the name of his friend, Arthur J. Moore. Bishop Moore was truly overwhelmed. For days he continued to express his surprise and his pleasure. He felt the Chair of Evangelism named in his honor was a confirmation of the central thrust of his ministry, an approval of what had always been in his opinion the main business of the church—to win others to Christ.

Among the programs of the South Georgia Conference is the annual "Winter Camp Meeting" usually held during the month of February at Epworth-By-The-Sea. A prominent preacher comes each year to lead in the week-long services. Bishop Earl G. Hunt, Jr. was the visiting preacher for the 1974 Winter Camp Meeting. But, the preaching hour on one day, February 7, was expressly reserved for Bishop Moore. The Winter Camp Meeting had designated this day as "Arthur J. Moore Day" to honor the Bishop. It was an important day for Bishop Moore; but for those who had known him in his prime and loved him, it was a painful day. Bishop Moore's health was visibly failing. Earlier in the week he had had a fall. I drove him the short distance from his room to the auditorium in order to save him from the strain of having to walk. His steps were unsure. His legs would become weak and might give way unexpectantly. He preached that day with all the vigor he could summon, but it was apparent to all who heard and saw him that Bishop Moore was nearing the end of the way. Increasingly he had come to forget words and phrases in his sermon and then to repeat himself. In the course of his sermon that day, he tried to speak to a familiar theme—the four dangers to spiritual religion. Soon it became obvious that he could not remember the third and fourth points. He would repeat the first two and come back to them again and again. But, regardless of how hard he tried, the third and fourth points would not come. His sermon that day was, I believe, the last time he stood to preach. Perhaps, deep inside, Bishop Moore also realized that there must come an end to even the best of things; and, although he still loved to preach, his preaching days were past.

Chapter 5
"TOWARDS THE LIGHT OF ETERNAL MORNING"

Bishop Moore's health was failing. It was obvious to all who knew him. It was painful to all who loved him. He had for so many years, and for so many people, been a tower of strength and source of boundless energy. His broad shoulders and robust build gave a countenance and look about him well-suited to the office of bishop. Bishop William R. Cannon would say later that he had a "bearing like that of General Zachary Taylor which impressed the public that he was born to command!" In short, Bishop Moore had always looked the part of a bishop. He told the story of stepping into an elevator one day in the city of Washington, D.C. The young man operating the elevator was visibly impressed by the bishop's demeanor. After a few moments, he turned to inquire, "Pardon me, sir, but are you by any chance a United States Senator?" To which Bishop Moore replied, "No, son, I'm not." A few moments later, he turned from his elevator controls again to ask, "Pardon me, sir, but are you by any chance the president of General Motors?" Again Bishop Moore replied, "No, I'm not." Not to be discouraged again, the young man asked, "Well, sir, just what are you?" The bishop replied, "I am a bishop of the Methodist Church." To which the young man responded, "Well, I didn't know exactly what you were, but I knew whatever you were you were the head of it!"

His personality was still commanding but more from respect for the man than from his physical bearing. Age was taking its toll. When I came to work for him in 1971, he had been suffering for some time from Parkinson's disease. Among its effects was the frequent, uncontrollable trembling of his hands which made writing extremely difficult.

73

Within a few months I began to take dictation from him in order to spare him as much as possible from having to write. His balance was at times unsteady and there was difficulty in walking. He frequently needed assistance especially in getting in and out of an automobile and going up and down steps. His physician, Dr. Byron Hoffman of the Roberts Memorial Clinic, insisted upon exercise to stimulate circulation in the Bishop's weakening legs. Unlike President Harry Truman, Bishop Moore had never been interested in the merits of walking. Dr. Hoffman suggested that he begin walking some each day. This, however, did not last too long. Other exercises which Dr. Hoffman prescribed did not last long either. Bishop Moore quickly grew weary of them. He either did not have the physical energy to exercise or he allowed a little pride to get in the way. He simply could not see the value for a man of his age and position to lie flat on his back and have his legs moved in a dozen different directions.

In October, 1973, Bishop Moore entered the Emory University Hospital in Atlanta, Georgia, for a week's stay. He stayed exactly seven days for a complete series of tests and x-rays. He hoped that perhaps something could be found to help him. He realized that his strength was failing. Perhaps he suspected a malignancy although he never mentioned it. There was no evidence of any malignancy found. He came home feeling, I think, relieved and a bit rejuvenated. He had been to the hospital, and nothing seriously wrong had been found. He felt better about himself. At least he knew that the problems he was having were the logical effects of age and the normal deterioration which accompanies the aging process.

The most difficult problem continued to be the weakness in his legs caused mainly by poor circulation. At times his legs would give way. The stairs to his upstairs bedroom became more and more difficult to climb. At one point Dr. Hoffman suggested that he use a walker around the house. However, when the Bishop was able to go, he always went almost at a run! The walker would consistently get in his way. So, he simply picked it up and carried it with him which was not the idea at all. Soon the walker found a corner where it stayed most of the time unless one of us insisted that the Bishop use it.

During the last years of his life, Bishop Moore's daily routine was regular. He usually rose between seven and eight in the morning. Mrs. Taylor would lay out his clothes for the day and sometimes helped him dress. In the last months of his life, I generally helped in this duty. He normally had breakfast about 8:30 a.m. Then, he would either read the morning paper, or watch television in his den, or work some in his upstairs office and study. When he was at home he took lunch promptly at noon. Then he retired to his bedroom for an afternoon nap which lasted anywhere from one to two hours. Following his nap, he would come down the hall to his office where we usually worked for several hours each afternoon. As I completed typing the day's correspondence, he normally went downstairs to his den to read or watch television. I would bring letters downstairs for his signature so that he would not have to climb the stairs again unnecessarily. He took his evening meal promptly at 5:00 p.m. Following dinner, he would watch the television news programs in the den. He retired early. Throughout his career he had made a practice of retiring early. He knew the value of plenty of rest. In the earlier days he used the evenings in his bedroom to read and study. He felt a need to get away from the crowd. He avoided evening engagements as much as possible. Even when he accepted them, he tried to be home and in his room early. He was a daylight person preferring luncheon engagements and planning his business so as to complete it during the day.

Being at home so much of the time during the last few years did not seem to bother him. Bishop Moore had traveled so much during his lifetime that he rather enjoyed being at home. He usually took his meals alone unless one of the children at home for a visit or I joined him. Wardlaw and his wife Lynda lived in the home as did their daughter and her family who had a basement apartment; however, their schedules did not fit in with the Bishop's. Both Wardlaw and Lynda worked outside the home. So, the Bishop was alone much of the time. Mrs. Blanche Taylor, the Moore's maid and cook for over thirty years, was in the home five days each week. She also made occasional trips to St. Simons Island with the Bishop especially to help with the House Parties.

By early 1974, it had become apparent that Bishop Moore's physical condition had worsened. He had had several unexplained falls. Once while in the kitchen I heard a noise overhead in his room. I went immediately upstairs to investigate. There I found him on the floor at the doorway to his bath unable to get up. He had no idea what had happened except that he found himself on the floor. His mind had been remarkably sound and keen. There were a few occasions when he seemed momentarily confused, at other times unable to remember. We attributed this to the poor circulation. However, it soon was apparent that the Bishop was having small, mild strokes—cerebral vascular accidents. This was not unusual in a person his age. There was no obvious paralysis. Apparently, the affected areas of the brain healed quickly or the damage thus far was negligible. There was nothing to be done which could prevent these mild strokes.

In February he began to have some difficulty with his vision. Two trips to the optometrist and some work on his glasses seemed to temporarily remedy the problem. During the following month, however, his vision became worse. I remember one afternoon towards the last of March, he said suddenly, "Something is wrong with my eyes; I can hardly see." An appointment was made immediately with Dr. Jess C. Lester, an Atlanta opthamologist, for April 3, 1974. Dr. Lester's examination supported what had been suspected all along. Bishop Moore had had a number of minor strokes. His field of vision had been significantly impaired by the brain damage from these strokes. Dr. Lester's charting of the bishop's field of vision showed the problem areas.

Still the bishop maintained an active schedule during that month of April. He attended a meeting of the Emory University Board of Trustees on April 4 and two days later went to Emory College at Oxford, Georgia, for an "Oxford

Day Celebration." Bishop Moore's daughter, Mrs. Evelyn Means, flew in from San Antonio, Texas, for a visit with her father. On April 10, I accompanied Bishop Moore to the Trust Company of Georgia Building in downtown Atlanta for a meeting of the Pitts Foundation. It was during this meeting that he submitted his resignation as Board Chairman. On Monday, April 15, Mrs. Alice Moore, Harry's widow, came from Americus, Georgia, for a visit. The week was spent pleasantly at home with Alice and Evelyn enjoying their visits. On Wednesday I drove them out to Westview Cemetery to visit Mrs. Moore's crypt in Westview Abbey. The architecturally striking mausoleum had been built by the late Asa G. Candler, Jr., a devoted friend and admirer of Bishop Moore's, who for a time owned and operated Westview Cemetery. Out of his love for the bishop, he had given him two places in the ornate mausoleum. Here Mrs. Moore's remains were entombed in 1964. The crypt directly above her's had been reserved for the Bishop. Two old friends came by during the week to visit, Dr. and Mrs. Sidney Anderson, who had both been missionaries in China. They had come within the last year to live in the Wesley Woods Retirement Center near the Emory University campus. On Saturday, Bishop Moore's sister, Kathleen, and half brother, Lee, came for a day's visit. Alice returned to Americus the following week, and Evelyn flew back to San Antonio on April 28. In retrospect it seems ironic and prophetic that the visits especially of these family members, Alice, Evelyn, Kathleen, and Lee, came as they did. We did not, of course, know it then, but it was to be the last time Bishop Moore was able to enjoy the presence of his family.

We were scheduled to leave for Epworth-By-The-Sea on Monday, April 29. Mrs. Taylor was to make the trip with us. The Board of Trustees of Epworth-By-The-Sea was to meet on Thursday, May 2. Bishop Moore had seen Dr. Hoffman for a check-up the previous week, and there seemed no reason not to make the trip to St. Simons. The drive down, however, was difficult. The bishop seemed very weak. He had to be helped in and out of the car at each stop. Upon arriving at the Methodist Center, he was unable to get out of the car without my virtually lifting him from the front seat. The result for me was a terrific sprain in my back which forced me to a hot tub and bed for the rest of the day and night. The next day Bishop Moore visited with two dear friends, Dr. and Mrs. George Clary. Dr. Clary, a contemporary of the Bishop's, had long been one of the leaders in the conference and had served at one time in the cabinet under Bishop Moore. On Thursday, I sat beside him for a meeting of the Epworth Board of Trustees. It was for him a long and exhausting meeting. However, he seemed refreshed by evening.

A dinner had been planned for six o'clock. Members of the Epworth Board, the South Georgia Conference Cabinet, and many friends of the bishop's had been invited. It was, in effect, another retirement occasion for Bishop Moore. He had decided to ask for release from his service on the Board at Epworth-By-The-Sea. It was his last "official retirement" from a responsibility with the church. More than one hundred and fifty persons had gathered to share in this testimonial dinner. Mr. Spencer Walden, a prominent Methodist layman and good friend from Albany, Georgia, presented a check to the bishop for several thousand dollars, a gift of love and appreciation from his many friends. There was a sharing time when some rose to express to the group their feelings about "what Bishop Moore had meant to them." It was a good occasion, well planned by the Reverend Vernard Robertson, the Superintendent of Epworth-By-The-Sea; Bishop Moore enjoyed himself immensely. Following the dinner, I walked with him to his room and helped him get ready for bed. He was tired but in good spirits as I said goodnight and went to my room nearby.

During the early morning hours something happened. When Mrs. Taylor arrived to help him get up and dress, she found him on the floor beside his bed. By the time I arrived, she had gotten him up, and the bishop was seated in a chair. He looked normal, but I detected immediately what appeared to be some paralysis in one arm. As he had so often, he immediately insisted that he was "fine," that there was nothing to worry about. We had planned to return to Atlanta that day, Friday, but I was frightened by the prospect of trying to make that long trip if, indeed, he was ill. The trip down had been difficult enough.

Upon the advice of several members of the staff at Epworth-By-The-Sea, and without Bishop Moore's knowledge, I called the office of Dr. John M. Smith, a young physician who practiced on St. Simons Island, and arranged through his nurse for him to meet us at the emergency room of the Glynn County Hospital just across the causeway in Brunswick. We had already packed for the return trip home. I did not know quite how the bishop would react to the arrangements I had made with the doctor's office. I told him that we would start out on the trip home, but for the sake of safety, we should stop by and check with a doctor in Brunswick before we got any further. I told him that I did not want to take any unnecessary chances with his health. Later, I would wish that we had just driven home that day. But, at the time, that did not seem the wisest thing to do. Surprisingly, he agreed to see the doctor in Brunswick.

Dr. Smith saw the bishop at the Glynn County Hospital. From his examination he concluded that the bishop had suffered a stroke. Upon Dr. Smith's advice, Bishop Moore agreed to be admitted to the hospital for the weekend for the purpose of observation. He was placed in an intensive care unit in order that he might have "around the clock" attention. Mrs. Taylor and I returned to Epworth-By-The-Sea for the weekend. I came to the hospital several times during the next two days to check on him. He was kept in bed for the weekend in order to rest.

On Monday morning, May 6, Bishop Moore was discharged from the hospital, and we began the trip home to Atlanta. Although he seemed in good spirits as we left Brunswick, he soon tired. He was weak, and the trip home became very difficult. Each time we stopped he tried to get in and out of the car and virtually collapsed in doing so. His legs simply gave way under him. We arrived home in the late afternoon, and quickly Mrs. Taylor and I put the bishop to bed. I was terribly uneasy and sat up most of the night watching him. The following morning when he awoke it was evident that he was completely disoriented. Perhaps there had been another stroke during the night. The events of the last three days were totally confused in his mind. Dr. Hoffman was called and began periodic visits to the home. He insisted that the bishop not be left alone day or night. The decision was made to hire private duty nurses in order to give him twenty-four-hour attention. I took one shift myself as well as keeping up with whatever business had to be cared for in the office.

By Friday, May 10, Bishop Moore's condition seemed somewhat improved. He was able to sit up a little. But, still, he could not understand what had happened to him. Everything that had taken place in the last week was confused in his mind. He could not sort out events or places or days. By May 14, it appeared that he had made a little further progress. Still very frail and weak, he could sit in a wheel chair. I would roll him to the office for a brief change of atmosphere, but even this would not last long. He would say, "I think I should lie down again." He tried to walk a little, but it was impossible without help on each side to hold him up. Even with help he quickly became exhausted. He was simply and frankly put, "worn out." Age, the accumulated effect of a long and full life of tireless labor, the years of travel and strain, had taken their toll.

There were a few visitors, usually persons he especially wanted to see, those who were the closest to him. I think he sensed that the end was closer now than it had ever been. Since returning home he had pleaded with us not to place him in the hospital. Although bedridden most of the time, he wanted to remain in his own home. One might say that he wanted to spend his last days in his own bed in the midst of familiar surroundings. Then, without warning, he changed his mind completely. I remember early one afternoon he looked directly at me and said, "I have been thinking: I should go over to the Emory University Hospital where perhaps they can do something to help me." We were all taken by surprise at this reversal in his attitude about going to the hospital. We realized the limitations of continuing to care for him at home. Now, he wanted to go, and Dr. Hoff-man seemed to feel that it was worth a try. At least in the hospital it would be possible to make a more thorough evaluation of his physical condition. Bishop Moore entered the Emory University Hospital on Thursday, May 23. It was necessary that he be moved by ambulance from his home to the hospital. I rode in the ambulance with him and at the hospital helped in completing the information necessary for his admission. He talked freely and lucidly with the ambulance attendants; he even promised them autographed copies of his autobiography.

Once in the hospital, however, his physical condition con-tinued to deteriorate. While his vital signs remained relatively strong for a man of his age, the accumulative brain damage from the many strokes was irreversible. There continued to be periods of mental confusion and disorienta-tion. In an effort to protect him, Dr. Hoffman insisted upon "no visitors."

The family had been concerned about securing someone to take my place. For several months I had planned to return to South Carolina at the end of May and to take an appoint-ment in the South Carolina Annual Conference. My degree work had been completed in mid-March at the Candler School of Theology. The Reverend Dave Hanson of the South Georgia Conference Program Council had recom-mended a young man, Steve Smith. Steve had had ex-perience in hospital and nursing care and seemed a good can-didate for the job to help care for Bishop Moore. In the last few weeks the secretarial duties had pretty much given way to nursing the bishop. I interviewed Steve in Albany, Georgia, on May 13. Plans were being made for him to come to Atlanta, live in the home, and help care for Bishop Moore after I left to return to South Carolina. However, after only a few days in the hospital, it was obvious to Wardlaw and to me that it would be impossible to care for the bishop at home again. Neither of us could know what the future would hold, but we were certain that the bishop could not come home again. Thus, the plans for Mr. Smith's employment were cancelled. We were both certain that for the remainder of the bishop's life he would have to be cared for in a skilled care nursing facility.

Several times in the first week of his confinement at Emory University Hospital he spoke to me about his own death. On one of those occasions he asked me to begin at once to plan for a series of memorial services in the different towns which had figured so prominently in his life and ministry—St. Simons Island, Argyle, Brookfield, Waycross, Atlanta. Of course, I knew that this was not what he really wanted done. However, I left his room that day promising to get right to the assignment he had given me. Fortunately, he never mentioned it again. He understood that I was leaving to return to South Carolina and to attend the meeting of my annual conference. The last time we spent together was on May 29. He rested a great deal of the time exhausted from even the smallest expenditure of energy. I promised him that I would come back to see him as soon as I could. "When you get back," he said, "we're going to hire a restaurant and have a big dinner party for all of our friends." As I was preparing to leave, he took my hand and said, "Son, I'm dying; when I'm gone, see that the service is kept triumphant and tell my family not to weep for me because it's not far to the Father's house." I closed the door to his room and stood outside in the hall briefly. I remember there was an ambiguous feeling of both relief and disappointment—relief that my responsibilities were at an end, at least I thought they were, and disappointment at not being able to share in the last leg of the journey. I wanted to be with him at the end, but, at the same time, I knew that there comes a time when one has to move on to something else and turn his face from what is past to what lies ahead. I had been privileged to share in a part of his life, to help him as a secretary, companion, and nurse. There is a limit to what any one person can do for another. My time was up.

Within roughly a week Wardlaw had moved his father from the Emory University Hospital to the Wesley Woods Nursing Center near Emory. The bishop's physical and mental condition continued to deteriorate. There was nothing medically that could be done to prevent it. Evelyn came from San Antonio to be with her father. Arthur, Jr., was ill in New York. By June 25, Bishop Moore's condition had deteriorated to the point that he did not recognize members of the family.

On Sunday afternoon, June 30, news programs across the nation brought word of the death of a prominent member of the Atlanta community. The name was known across the nation. Mrs. Martin Luther King, Sr., had been fatally wounded in a shooting at the Ebenezer Baptist Church in Atlanta. The nation was shocked by word of the tragedy. A man in the congregation at the church that morning suddenly went on a shooting spree. Mrs. King was among the victims. By evening another prominent and well-known member of the Atlanta community had died. Quietly, at the age of 85 years, Bishop Arthur J. Moore, the race won, the good fight fought, and the faith kept, slipped away into that "blessed sleep from which none ever wakes to weep." Months earlier during a visit with an old friend and colleague, Bishop Edward L. Tullis, Bishop Moore had repeated what Bishop A. Frank Smith had once said about facing death. "No, I'm not afraid to die," Bishop Frank Smith had said, "but I have some concern that I may have a hard struggle getting out of this body." Bishop Moore's struggle was short-lived, and those who knew him and loved him were so thankful that this man who had served so vigorously and dynamically did not have to linger needlessly and helplessly month after month. In an interview for *The Atlanta Constitution* in 1973, he had said:

> I'm ready to die, not in any boastful sort of way, but because I am an ardent believer in personal and instant immortality. I don't believe that God can be good and kind and merciful to someone who has served him faithfully and just let death cut off all that communion and let you drop into oblivion.[13]

Characteristically, Bishop Moore had outlined the arrangements for his own funeral years earlier. In December, 1971, he had handed me the rough draft of a letter addressed to his family which he asked me to type and date, "December 26, 1971"—the day of his eighty-third birthday.

In the letter he asked that the service be held at Glenn Memorial Church at the Emory University Campus and that the time of the service be placed "far enough ahead" so that "any of my friends who desire to come will have time to do so." He had asked that Bishop William R. Cannon and Bishop Earl G. Hunt, Jr., be among those to lead the service. At the time of the Bishop's death, both Bishops Cannon and Hunt were with a continuing education group in Scotland. Bishop Hunt did not feel he could come due to illness in his group from the Western North Carolina Conference. It was agreed among the bishops there that Bishop Cannon would return while the remaining bishops would assume Bishop Cannon's responsibilities in Scotland.

In his letter Bishop Moore had written, "keep the service bright and triumphant." He requested specifically two hymns, "Jesus, I My Cross Have Taken" and the great hymn of Charles Wesley, "Thou Hidden Source of Calm Repose." Many months before his last illness, Bishop Moore had asked a close friend, the Reverend Ray Vaughn, to sing. For the service, Ray arranged a beautiful medley of "Amazing Grace" and "Marvellous Grace of Our Blessed Lord." The family asked Dr. Bevel Jones, Bishop Nolan B. Harmon, and Dr. Louie D. Newton, whom Bishop Moore had named in his letter, to share in the service. Bishop Cannon, en route from Scotland, would deliver the sermon and eulogy. Mrs. Ellen Kizer and the Reverend William L. Cawthon would serve as organists. The Reverend Herchel H. Sheets, Minister of Teaching and Administration at Glenn Memorial Church, was most helpful in the arrangements at the church. Dr. Bevel Jones, in consultation with the other participants in the service, arranged the order of worship which included the two hymns Bishop Moore had requested and an additional selection, "A Mighty Fortress Is Our God." As Bishop Moore had requested, the pallbearers were selected from preachers and laymen of the North and South Georgia Annual Conferences: Mr. A. J. Strickland, III, the Reverend Charles R. Williams, the Reverend William R. Ruff, the Reverend Gordon Thompson, Mr. Henry L. Bowden, the Reverend Guy Hutcherson, the Reverend C. E. Steele, the Reverend W. A. Tyson, Jr. Members of the Council of Bishops, The Ten Club, and members of the North and South Georgia Annual Conferences formed the escort of honorary pallbearers.

Friends from across Georgia and the nation gathered for the service of "faith and triumph" at 11:00, Wednesday morning, July 3, in the sanctuary of Glenn Memorial United Methodist Church. Mrs. Jimmy Carter attended representing the State of Georgia while her husband, the Governor, attended the services for Mrs. Martin Luther King, Sr. As the organ pealed forth the soul stirring chords of "Jesus I My Cross Have Taken," and the congregation reached the familiar words,

> Perish every fond ambition,
> All I've sought or hoped or known;
> Yet how rich is my condition:
> God and heaven are still my own!

I could not help but feel how much the bishop would have liked this service. In his personal words of tribute to his friend, Dr. Louie D. Newton said of Bishop Moore: "That vibrant voice is silent here; that lucid pen moves no more across the page; but every evening star will remind us that his spirit goes marching on in countless hearts around the globe and he awaits us yonder in the land and life beyond where the flowers never wilt and the congregation is never dismissed, in God's house forever."

Among the items in the "letter to his family," which Bishop Moore prepared in 1971, was a statement which he wished read at his funeral service. He had first penned these paragraphs years earlier as a response to the occasion of his retirement. He included them in his autobiography. The closing paragraph of the statement spoke eloquently of his belief in immortality.

> The Methodist Church has laid upon my shoulders many responsibilities, but it has also given to me a great many honors. Perhaps no man ever stood seeking admission at the bar of an Annual Conference with so little to offer as credentials of his worthiness for the work of the ministry. But, in great kindness, the South Georgia Conference received me "on trial" in 1909.

From that humble circuit to which I was sent in that year, I have traveled a world-wide circuit and had the privilege of being the "Ambassador" of Methodism upon almost every continent of the earth.

God hath set the eternal in our hearts. He makes the seen and the unseen one. He bridges the gulf between a world that now is and the eternal world of abiding beauty. We are neither guests of a night nor captives of a cruel world, but children in the family of God. That broken sepulcher in Joseph's garden assures us that God hath set the light of immortality in our hearts and not even death can put it out. Our Christian faith is never so confident, never so triumphant as when it proclaims the everlasting life. We march, not toward the setting sun, but toward the light of morning; the light that shineth more and more unto the perfect day. This life and the next are one and what God hath joined together, let not man put asunder.

The light that falls upon my pathway is the light of Eternal Morning.

Arthur J. Moore

Chapter 6
ASSOCIATIONS

Across his long episcopal career Bishop Moore came to be associated with prominent leaders in the affairs of both the church and the state. He was known in many places in the United States and around the world. His work as a bishop in so many different countries brought him into contact with military, political, as well as religious leadership.

In June, 1973, when Dr. Billy Graham came to Atlanta, Georgia, for a crusade, Bishop Moore was invited to deliver the invocation at the opening service of the crusade. During the week of the crusade Dr. Graham called on Bishop Moore at his home and enjoyed a morning visit with him. Their friendship had begun many years earlier during the first Billy Graham Atlanta Crusade. Dr. Graham was then not as well known as he is today and the prospects for that first crusade in Atlanta were not good. Bishop Moore came out publicly in support of the services, urged Methodists to attend and participate, and is credited with having significantly contributed to the positive response which the crusade received.

Bishop Moore's associations with other internationally known religious leaders were numerous. They included Dr. John R. Mott, E. Stanley Jones, and Toyohiko Kagawa whom he visited in Japan. Bishop Moore spoke frequently and admiringly of Dr. William E. Sangster of England, whom he considered to be one of the world's great preachers. Dr. Sangster's dream, according to Bishop Moore, was to see a revival of vital and vigorous Methodism in England; he did not live to see his dream realized. Among Bishop Moore's friends and associates was Dr. Norman Vincent Peale. Their admiration and respect for each other was mutual. Upon the occasion of Bishop Moore's death, Dr. Peale wrote: "I was devoted to him and shall never forget him. He had a great impact on my life as he did on so many others." Dr. Peale had done the narration for the film on Bishop Moore's life produced by the University of Georgia's Center For Continuing Education. Bishop Moore had written Dr. Peale thanking him for this and, in return, received the following reply:

> Dear Arthur:
>
> Thank you so much for your letter of June 29.
>
> I did indeed have the privilege and pleasure of helping to make that marvelous documentary film on your great life and ministry.
>
> As I narrated the story I found myself being deeply moved by the narrative, with which I was so familiar, how as a poor boy you had the call to preach the Gospel. And how well you did it, and the lives you touched, and the great outstanding religious leader you became. It was all very moving.
>
> I have always held you in great admiration and affection. You are just the greatest, and I have never heard a person in my life who can move the human heart as you can do. I only hope to have the pleasure of seeing you again one of these days.
>
> With sincere affection, in which Ruth joins, I am, as always,
>
> Cordially,
>
> Norman[14]

Among the leadership of the Methodist church, Bishop Moore perhaps knew more men and women across a longer span of time than any other single person. The missionaries were always special to him. Indeed, when one of the retired officers in the area of missionary personnel whom the bishop first came to work with in the Methodist Episcopal Church, South, died, the minister who was to conduct her funeral service called Bishop Moore for help in putting together a fitting eulogy. Her contemporaries were all deceased, and there was literally no one left who "went back" that far, except Bishop Arthur J. Moore.

Bishop Moore played a part in shaping the ministries of such men as Harry Denman and Grover C. Emmons. He was among the leadership which selected and called Dr. Denman to be the first General Secretary of the Board of Evangelism. As a member of the staff of the Board of Missions, Grover C. Emmons designed *The Upper Room* which has become one of the great contributions of the Methodist church to the devotional life of people around the world. Among the bishop's closest friends across the years was Homer Rodeheaver. "Rody" had succeeded Fred Fischer in 1909 as Billy Sunday's music leader. The Rodeheaver Gospel Publishing Company of Winona Lake, Indiana, supplied gospel hymnals for churches everywhere. Generations were raised on the Rodeheaver "shaped note" edition. Homer Rodeheaver was an evangelist and musician. In the 1930's Homer Rodeheaver accompanied Bishop Moore on one of the earliest and still experimental air flights from Brussels, Belgium, to the Congo. The trip lasted six days with the plane landing usually at army outposts. The flight took them across the vastness of the Sahara Desert. There was a third man on the flight who according to Bishop Moore, "wrote out his last will and testament." "Rody," said Bishop Moore, "passed out chewing gum." When Homer Rodeheaver died, Bishop Moore traveled a long distance to be present for his funeral service and to pay his respects to his friend in a beautiful eulogy and sermon.

Bishop Moore's associations with the bishops of his church reached all the way from Bishop H. C. Morrison, whom he had invited as a young preacher to dedicate the new church in Townsend, Georgia, in 1910, to the last classes elected during the jurisdictional conferences of 1972. Of the bishops he knew, William Newman Ainsworth had the greatest impact upon his life. In *Bishop To All Peoples* Bishop Moore wrote, "As far as I can tabulate the facts, I am more heavily in the debt of this great and good man than any other single person."[15] Dr. Ainsworth, first as a fellow minister and then as a bishop, had become a "spiritual father" to Arthur J. Moore. He encouraged him and urged other ministers to invite him for revival meetings. Bishop

Ainsworth saw in the preaching of Arthur Moore something vital and full of life which the church needed to hear. Later, as a bishop, Dr. Ainsworth placed him in his first settled pastorate. Following Bishop Ainsworth's death, Bishop Moore was among those who worked to see that Bishop Ainsworth's ministry was not forgotten and that the name of this native son should be revered by Georgia Methodists.

Two of his episcopal colleagues were always especially close to him—Bishop Paul B. Kern and A. Frank Smith. Bishop Moore would often say, "We were young together." Elected together, these three men were for many years the youngest bishops serving the work of the Methodist Episcopal Church, South. It was natural that they found companionship in each other. Bishop Moore said of Bishop A. Frank Smith that he was a man of great persuasive power. "A. Frank Smith," Bishop Moore would say jokingly, "could convince a convicted man on his way to the death chamber that he was rendering his country an invaluable service." In one of those letters which a person comes to cherish and keep in a special place, Bishop A. Frank Smith wrote to Bishop Moore on April 12, 1960: "I thank God for the providence that brought us together in the beginning of our ministry. No other person has ever influenced my life as have you."

One of the best descriptions of the power of Bishop Moore's ministry came from another of his episcopal colleagues, Bishop G. Bromley Oxnam. In a letter dated January 14, 1949, Bishop Oxnam wrote the following:

> I have never been able to tell you really how much your leadership means to us all. You do something for each one of us in the realm of the spirit that cannot be expressed in words. I have often tried to analyze it, but have given up, since it forbids analysis. So often when you speak, I find myself under a strange, almost hypnotic spell. That is not the way to express it at all, because it doesn't lie in that realm. I can say it better, I think, when I take the older religious terminology and speak very frankly of the presence of the Holy Spirit. Your devotional addresses always lift us, and the consuming passion which has ruled your life is communicated to us with all its warmth and transforming power.[16]

Bishop Moore's work often brought him into contact with heads of governments and others in prominent political positions. In the countries to which he was assigned, it was his practice to seek out the leaders in the government in an effort to understand the country's official attitude toward religious work and to determine what the church's future might be under that particular administration. In Korea in the 1930's he came to know General Jiro Minami who ran Korea as Japanese governor general and with whom the church, for better or worse, had to deal. After World War II, Bishop Moore saw General Minami again as a war criminal reduced to coarse P.O.W. garb. He had once ruled Korea in the splendor of an eastern despot. Through his work in Korea after World War II, Bishop Moore came to be associated with Syngman Rhee whose career he had observed and which he respected for his opposition to Japanese tyranny and his desire to build a democratic Korea.

Bishop Moore's closest friends among the political leaders in Asia were Generalissimo and Madame Chiang Kai-shek. To the end of his life, Bishop Moore maintained his sympathy and support for the Chiangs. He never lost his confidence in them or his belief in the battle which they were waging against the forces of communism. Madame Chiang, Mei-ling Soong, was educated at Wesleyan College in Macon, Georgia. She helped to lead her husband to Christ. Together, as Methodists, they greatly supported and helped the church in China. The New Life Movement begun in 1934 by Chiang Kai-shek was influenced by his recently accepted Christianity. After the fall of the Nationalist Government on the mainland in 1949, Bishop Moore continued his support for the Chiangs. Some seven letters from Madame Chiang Kai-shek are in the Moore Archives at Epworth-By-The-Sea. Bishop Moore believed the Chiangs to be the only hope for a free China in the face of mounting communist aggression and, later, that the presence of their government on Taiwan offered the only alternative to China completely under the control of the communists.

Taipei, Taiwan
May 7, 1955

Dear Bishop Moore:

Thank you for your reassuring letter of April 16th. Letters from staunch friends, like your good self, of China and of truth and justice, do indeed encourage and enhearten us in crucial days like these.

We need the continuing interest and prayers of Christian people. Do you know the verse, anonymous as far as I am aware:
"We cannot tell how often as we pray
For some bewildered one, hurt and distressed,
The answer comes—but many times these hearts
Find sudden peace and rest."

You express your desire to render any possible service. I am sure your clear voice and facile pen are constantly employed in the cause of justice and righteousness. It is only those, like yourself, with perceptive mind and the courage of conviction, who can answer such specious arguments as those advanced recently by a group of fourteen Protestant Church leaders to President Eisenhower. Someone sent me the clipping from the NEW YORK TIMES of Sunday, April 3rd. The letter confuses Free China's desire to keep faith with the free peoples (some 60,000 civilians alone) on the offshore islands, to keep up the hope of mainland millions for eventual liberation, and to hold the allegiance of some 12,000,000 overseas Chinese, with a selfish desire to "save face." How can Christian leaders think so little of moral principles? And can't they realize that only firmness on the part of the West will keep the Asian peoples from climbing on to what looks like the band wagon of Communist success?

Again, thanking you for your good wishes and prayers.

Yours sincerely,

Madame Chiang Kai-shek[17]

During the last years of his life as pressure in the United States mounted for the recognition of the People's Republic of China, Bishop Moore's faith in the Nationalist Government on Taiwan remained strong. To desert that government was, in his opinion, morally wrong.

Following the Second World War, Bishop Moore found a helpful friend in the person of General Lucius D. Clay. General Clay, a native Georgian, served as Commander of United States Armed Forces in Europe from 1947 to 1949. With General Clay's help, Bishop Moore was able to travel about Germany to visit Methodist work. General Clay also made it possible for the bishop to fly into Berlin on one of the planes involved in the Berlin Airlift. In Japan, General Douglas MacArthur received the Bishop at his head-quarters in Tokyo and soon became a helpful friend. To be around General MacArthur, Bishop Moore related, was like being in the presence of royalty. Every time the General went somewhere, it was as if he moved to the flourish of trumpets and the waving of flags. It was General Mac-Arthur who arranged for Bishop Moore to visit Jiro Minami in prison.

One of Bishop Moore's most memorable meetings with a prominent figure in government took place with United States Secretary of State, Cordell Hull. Returning from a trip to Asia where he had seen first hand the Japanese invasion of China and the brutality of war, Bishop Moore called upon Mr. Hull to protest the United States failure to intervene to prevent such blatant aggression. Mr. Hull replied frankly that when he came to the Office of Secretary of State he found this nation deeply entrenched in isola-tionism and that he had to deal with the nation where it was. And, he added, that the "gentlemen of the clergy" had as much to do as any other group with leading this country into the isolationism which paralyzed its foreign policy.

Occasionally the Council of Bishops would meet with the President of the United States. One concluding story I wish to relate concerned a visit of the Council of Bishops to the office of President Franklin D. Roosevelt. According to Bishop Moore, no one in the group had to worry about who would "carry the conversation" around Mr. Roosevelt. He did! President Roosevelt mentioned the fact that already the Catholic church had Cardinal Spellman visiting the war front. Looking directly at Bishop Adna W. Leonard, whom the President knew by name, Mr. Roosevelt raised the question as to what *we protestants* were going to do. According to Bishop Moore, Bishop Leonard "snapped to attention" as if it were a personal challenge. And, within a few weeks, he was off on a visit to the war front. Bishop Leonard never reached the war zone, however; his plane crashed en route and he was killed.

Arthur J. Moore saw his ministry in world terms. The variety of his associations testify to this. Although for many years a conspicuous leader of "southern" Methodism, Bishop Moore did not think of himself as a purely sectional leader. His ministry had a national as well as international dimension. He learned through his associations with others at home and abroad and saw first-hand the history which now we can only read about. His associations and experiences with Christians and non-Christians throughout the world expanded his vision and served to strengthen his conviction that the answer to the deepest needs of nations and people everywhere could only be found in Jesus Christ.

Chapter 7
UNDERSTANDING THE MAN

In an interview for *The Emory Alumnus* magazine Bishop Arthur J. Moore once said, "There are four chief facts about my life: I had honest parents, I married a wonderful girl, I got religion, and I worked hard." Such a brief statement touches the high points of his life, but it fails to give a complete picture of the real Arthur J. Moore. What made him the man that he was? How do we account for his remarkable life?

At the beginning it should be said that Arthur J. Moore was born and reared in a Christian home. There the foundations of his life were laid sturdy and deep. He idealized his parents. He never disdained the teaching and training which he received at their hands. His memories of his childhood were good memories rich in things of the Spirit. He spoke of their influence upon his life with abiding gratitude. His upbringing took place in an atmosphere of hard work but of cheerfulness and joy as well. The simple pleasures of life were the rule in his childhood home.

It was, therefore, not surprising that the positive influences of childhood would one day merge with the vitality of a religious experience. He would later describe himself as a "miracle of grace." That grace was truly "prevenient." Arthur Moore knew the Christian life. The decisive moment came when he himself chose to make Christ the single ultimate allegiance of his life. He was by nature adventurous. Beginning with the moment he committed his life to Christ, following Christ became an adventure. He never grew weary of it. He was the kind of a man who could give himself wholeheartedly to a cause without any reservation. An old friend May East Keller, who with Charlie Tillman and Jewel

Tillman Burns shared in an evangelistic team with Arthur Moore in the very early years of his ministry, said of Bishop Moore, "To me he was a living example of what God can do with a man who gives his all—leaving the forgiven sins behind."

Bishop Moore's lack of a formal education has often been pointed out. He readily confessed that he did not have first-rate educational qualifications and that he came into the ministry ill-equipped educationally. When Arthur J. Moore was born, society offered little in the way of public education. Facilities and personnel were limited. As a young person he took advantage of all that public education offered him in his home village. It was as much as many young men of his day received. Of course, it was nowhere near the standards of today. But, it was a beginning. Later, enrolled for a year as a special student in Emory College at Oxford, Georgia, he received his first and only exposure to a college curriculum. More important, however, there he came under the influence of certain teachers who inspired in him a love for learning, which subsequently became a great force in his life.

What Arthur Moore lacked in formal preparation, he more than made up for in a passion for reading and learning through personal study. He read, and he listened. He learned to preach by listening. Whenever he could, he went to hear other preachers; and, as his travel widened, he would go to hear the great preachers and speakers of his day and to learn from them. He was determined to learn and to personally compensate for a lack of earned college degrees. He became one of the most knowledgeable men in his generation through self-education. He lived with books, and his reading was spent with the best literature, the great books by the leading authors in religion and history. Bishop William R. Cannon, in his funeral eulogy of Bishop Moore, said, "he feasted on great thoughts." He gave his mental energy and time, not to the petty, trivial issues of the moment, but to the lasting ideas, the eternal truths around which men and women throughout recorded history have centered their hopes and aspirations. His sermons were always centered around the central themes of the Christian gospel, the abiding truths, the everlasting certainties.

Books, his love for reading, and his love of learning shaped his life and language. In later years when he gave his personal library to the Methodist Museum at Epworth-By-The-Sea, it numbered several thousand volumes. The man who never earned a college degree received honorary doctorates from eight colleges and universities: Asbury College in Kentucky, Central College in Missouri, Southwestern University in Texas, Randolph Macon College in Virginia, Florida Southern College in Florida, and Emory University, Mercer University, and Paine College in Georgia. His published writings included three mission study books: *The Sound of Trumpets, Christ After Chaos: The Post-War Policy of the Methodist Church in Foreign Lands,* and *Christ and Our Country: The Missionary Evangelization of the U. S. A.*; four volumes of sermons: *Central Certainties, Immortal Tidings in Mortal Hands, The Mighty Savior,* and *Fight On! Fear Not!*; and his autobiography, *Bishop To All Peoples.*

The greatest single influence of another person in shaping his life came unquestionably from his beloved wife, Martha McDonald Moore. They shared fifty-eight years as husband and wife. In the opinion of many, she was always the "power behind the bishop." Martha Moore was a vast reservoir of spiritual strength and physical determination. She stood strongly behind her husband. When the going became hard, she was there to restore his spirits. Never complaining about his long absences from home, she molded the family and managed the household, always allowing the bishop to believe that he was the "head of house." The stability which Mrs. Moore brought to the family made it possible for the bishop to fulfill his responsibilities around the world. They worked well as a team.

She was his source of inspiration. The bishop once inscribed the statement to her that "she was the bright star in his life leading him homeward from his travels in faraway lands." Mrs. Moore was a devout Christian who gave a constant witness to the redemptive power of Christ. She never became angry or grew disheartened. No problem was too much for her. She loved people and befriended everyone. The bishop preached the gospel. Mrs. Moore lived it. She supported her husband in all that he wanted to do. By quiet example she challenged him to be the best that he was capable of being. It is not unfair to say that in her own unique way as a mother and homemaker she made it possible for her husband to rise to greatness.

Arthur J. Moore gave himself totally to the church. It was not, however, without great personal sacrifice. In his later years Bishop Moore would reveal that the one regret he had in his ministry was that his service as a bishop took him away from home and family so much. The separation from his wife and children especially during the children's growing-up years was the price he had to pay for a ministry in a world-wide parish. The bishop was proud of his children. However, he was never able to recapture what the years of separation and travel had cost him in the loss of family and home life.

Arthur Moore's roots were in the soil of south Georgia. He never forgot that. In the final analysis Bishop Arthur J. Moore was a "Son of Georgia." His heart was always there. He traveled a world-wide circuit, but he never forgot where he was born or the people who nurtured him on his way to a place of prominence in World Methodism. In his last years there was something which drew him time and again to south Georgia. As we traveled the highways and byways of that part of his native state, every town brought to his memory some story out of the past, some vivid memory of people and events which shaped the religious and political life of Georgia. In his last years his heart yearned often to journey again to the area in southern Georgia where he was born and grew up; to Argyle the place of his birth, to Brookfield where he lived as a child, to Willachoochie where he and his beloved Martha were married, to Waycross where he was converted. Bishop Moore crossed the oceans almost one hundred times, but he was always a Son of Georgia. Each town, each crossroads held a story. To ride in a car through south Georgia with Bishop Moore was to hear an oral history of Methodism in Georgia. Each place brought forth personal recollections of conferences and meetings, of events and people out of the past.

Arthur J. Moore bridged the gulf between two centuries. He was a product of the reconstruction South and knew well its deprivations. He knew equally well the customs and traditions of the "Old South" and cherished them. However, he was called to live out his ministry and service in the twentieth century. He saw the needs of the future, especially the need to grow beyond sectionalism and to deal as Christians with the social issues of the times. His was a skillful balancing act—to stand with one foot in the nineteenth century, cherishing the past, and the other foot in the twentieth century, working constructively to meet change in a spirit of Christian love and brotherhood. He possessed a great appreciation for the past. He participated in history, and sensed profoundly his participation in history. Those who today would criticize him for not taking a more active role in such a social issue as race, for example, must remember that *for his time and generation*, he was a leader in working for better race relations. He spoke to the social issues of his time but always as a product of the South and always in the light of the historical background of Methodism—namely, that a transformation of society comes through transformed hearts.

Bishop Arthur J. Moore was the last of an era in the episcopal history of the Methodist Episcopal Church, South. Among the bishops of the southern church only Bishop Will C. Martin survived him. Bishop Martin was elected in 1938, with the Plan of Union already adopted and unification at hand. So, it is fair to say that Bishop Arthur J. Moore was the last bishop of the Methodist Episcopal Church, South. He personified the best qualities of the church, South. A gentlemanly graciousness of manner, an allegiance to tradition and custom, a belief in evangelism as the main business of the church, the "warm heart," a commitment to maintaining the balance between the experience and expression of religion, a native pride in the religious institutions of the South, a belief in the power of the pulpit

99

and the centrality of preaching in the worship of the church, a cautious attitude toward change—these were the ingredients which blended in his making as a preacher and a bishop of the Methodist Episcopal Church, South. It is impossible to understand him apart from this tradition.

He never systematically set down his views concerning the episcopal office, but it is sufficient to say that they were in large part formed by the traditions of the Methodist Episcopal Church, South. Without intending any disrespect, it is possible to say that Arthur J. Moore was the last of the "imperial episcopacy" in the southern branch of Methodism. To Arthur Moore the Office of Bishop was substantially more than an administrative position. It was a symbol of the church itself. The bishop was a spiritual leader and pastor to all those under his charge. He led; others followed. He spoke; others listened. Someone once said that at a gathering or dinner one would not know where the "head table" was until Bishop Moore arrived; it was where he sat! The Office of Bishop was a rallying point of morale and spirit for the church. It was not so much the man "Arthur Moore" who craved the glory, though we all have some desire for a little glory in life; it was, rather, the man in the Office of Bishop who sought the honor for the sake of the office. Arthur Moore had an exalted view of the episcopacy because he knew that people needed a figure in whom they could place their trust and to whom they could look for guidance and direction.

Arthur J. Moore looked the part of a bishop. He carried himself in such a way as to complement the dignity of the office. In a very positive sense he was among those who made the Office of Bishop a source of power and strength for the church. Through the authority of the episcopal office, he was able to accomplish things for the church when no one else could or would. When he first acquired the name, "King Arthur," it was out of appreciation and respect. As a young bishop, he possessed both the youth and the vitality to "seize the day" and to serve in difficult and demanding places of need. As he grew older, a few critics called him authoritarian and paternalistic. It would be more accurate to say that he took seriously the role which he understood to be his in the life of the church and he knew the value of being decisive. In meeting the problems before it, the church needed a "sure" word and a sense of the imperative. That required a single-mindedness of purpose and will. Arthur Moore brought that kind of decisiveness and commitment to his work as a bishop.

To understand Arthur J. Moore one must understand that he was a churchman. The church received him into the ministry when he had very little to offer in the way of experience or preparation. The church accepted him when he felt himself the least acceptable. He never forgot this. His life's work was the church. When it called, he answered. Wherever it sent him, he went. Throughout the last years of his life, Bishop Moore maintained an active interest in the affairs of the church. Whenever possible, he attended meetings of the Council of Bishops. He received and read numerous church publications. He especially looked forward to receiving *Newscope* published by the United Methodist Publishing House and a weekly news release published by United Methodist Communications, two publications which brought concise and up-to-date news of happenings throughout the church. In the last few years of his life, two issues touched him most deeply.

The first issue concerned the growing divisiveness between the more evangelistically oriented membership of the church and the church's established boards and agencies which tended to be more liberal in their approaches to Christian social concerns. He feared the growth of the Good News Movement as a separate, competing movement within the life of the church. To Arthur Moore the experience and the expression of religion were inseparable. Ond could not be understood apart from the other. The other issue which deeply concerned him centered around the situation at Pikeville, Kentucky, involving striking employees at a Methodist institution. Bishop Moore was concerned about the role which the Council of Bishops considered playing in this situation. He was especially concerned that the Council of Bishops not become an arbitrating body in the dispute.

101

He was also fearful that the Council of Bishops might open its meetings to the press and public in efforts to mediate disputes and resolve problems. If the Council did this, he contended, it would lose its deliberative character.

Arthur J. Moore was not a theologian in the academic sense. He dedicated his life and ministry to proclaiming the gospel and especially to proclaiming the basic, most central tenets of Christianity. He has been described as "an orthodox evangelical liberal with a forward looking attitude." Bishop Moore came a little "closer to the point" in describing himself theologically. He once said, "I am conservative as to the content of my faith but adventuresome in what I do with it." He described Christianity as the "love for one unique person, Jesus Christ." He was a vigorous exponent of evangelical Christianity. The church has a message and a mission for all the world. It must venture out from its marble altars and beautiful sanctuaries into the world. "A Church that neglects the masses," he once said, "will not dominate the tomorrows."

He was a tower of strength, and a symbol of stability. He served the Church so long that often just to see him brought a feeling of reassurance that "God was still in his heavens and all was right with the world." But, equally important, he possessed a deep humanity. He identified with the suffering of people. As a churchman, he worked in the interests of those institutions and agencies which responded to human need. He knew the importance of opportunity, especially educational opportunity. He gave his time and energy in many different places to see that young people had the advantage of formal education which he, himself, had lacked. It was an unspoken but deeply personal goal of his life's work to leave for those who came after him something of value and beauty, something which stimulated the mind and uplifted the heart.

One is tempted to say that Arthur Moore was a poor boy from south Georgia who made good. Such a statement needs some amplification. He was poor materially; his family's means were modest. He was born in a time and place which provided little in the way of economic and educational opportunities. Such circumstances did not leave him bitter but rather eager and grateful for the opportunities that did come to him. He made good, but he never forgot that he made good through the grace of God and through the caring and interest of other people.

Perhaps his greatest legacy to the church was that he had a world view of Christianity. The missionary enterprise was the great interest of his life. Beginning with the time as a young man when he wanted to go to Korea as a missionary until the end of his life, he never lost sight of the world mission of the church. He would say that if Christ is not for every country, every people, then we have made Christ less than what he is. He lived his life convinced that the Christian message was adequate and universal. The missionary enterprise, international evangelism, was the great adventure of the church. He never lost his enthusiasm for that adventure.

> The Church can never regard itself as spiritually sound without an adequate missionary program. The passion to share Christ with our brothers everywhere is the authentic and inevitable outcome of Christian experience. We must carry the good news, not only to obey an external command, but because we who have found Christ are captives of an inner necessity which drives us forth to express that glorious fact.[18]

For Arthur J. Moore the banners of the faith were always unfurled, and the church like the valiant prince in an ancient legend was always riding forth to do battle with the forces of evil and indifference. Bishop Moore kept before the church a world view of Christianity which pointed beyond provincialism and narrow nationalism to a universal brotherhood of man under the Lordship of Christ. The preaching of the gospel, he once wrote, is not for one time and place but for every age and every place.

POSTSCRIPT

On December 28, 1974, in ceremonies at the Georgia State Capitol Building in Atlanta, a portrait of Bishop Arthur J. Moore was presented to the State of Georgia to hang in the capitol rotunda among the portraits of other famous Georgians. The man who, as a minister of the Gospel of Jesus Christ, had served a world-wide parish, the "Ambassador of Methodism" to the far corners of the world, was on that day honored as a son of the Georgia he loved.

NOTES

1. Proceedings of the Southeastern Jurisdictional Conference of the United Methodist Church, *Daily Christian Advocate*, 16 July 1972, (Waynesville, North Carolina), p. 4.
2. *Ibid.*, p. 5.
3. Arthur J. Moore, *Bishop To All Peoples* (Nashville: Abingdon Press, 1973), p. 32.
4. *Ibid.*, p. 52.
5. *Ibid.*, p. 66.
6. *Ibid.*, p. 78.
7. Translation of a letter from the Japanese Embassy, Moore Collection, The Methodist Museum, Epworth-By-The-Sea. Used by permission.
8. *Bishop To All Peoples*, p. 110.
9. "The Address of the Council of Bishops," *Daily Christian Advocate*, 27 April 1944, (Kansas City, Missouri), p. 26.
10. *Ibid.*, p. 31.
11. *Ibid.*, p. 36.
12. *Bishop To All Peoples*, p. 59ff.
13. *The Atlanta Constituion*, Friday, 4 May 1973.
14. Letter by Norman Vincent Peale is used by permission of Norman Vincent Peale.
15. *Bishop To All Peoples*, p. 130.
16. Letter by Bishop Oxnam, Moore Collection, The Methodist Museum, Epworth-By-The-Sea. Used by permission.
17. Letter by Madame Chiang Kai-shek, Moore Collection, The Methodist Museum, Epworth-By-The-Sea. Used by permission.
18. Arthur J. Moore, *Apathy or Advance* (Nashville: Board of Missions, 1935), pp. 26-27.

ABOUT THE AUTHOR

Roger M. Gramling is a native of Orangeburg, South Carolina. He holds the A.B. Degree from Pfeiffer College, Misenheimer, North Carolina, and the Master of Divinity Degree from Emory University, Atlanta, Georgia. While at Pfeiffer, he served as President of the Student Government Association and was the first student representative in the college's history to sit on its Board of Trustees.

From 1971-1974, in addition to his studies at Emory University's Candler School of Theology, he was employed as personal secretary to the late Arthur J. Moore, Senior Bishop of the United Methodist Church. He assisted in preparing and editing the final manuscript of Bishop Moore's autobiography.

Gramling has been a member of the South Carolina Annual Conference since 1972. He served Saint John's United Methodist Church in Rock Hill, South Carolina, as Associate Minister from 1974-1977. Active in the Rock Hill Christian Minister's Association, he served on its Executive Committee for two years as Director of Public Relations and Radio Ministry.

In June, 1977, he was appointed to the Latimer Memorial United Methodist Church in Belton, South Carolina, where he presently serves. He is active in numerous civic organizations. He presently serves on the Anderson District Council on Ministries of the United Methodist Church and is a member of the Program Planning Committee of the South Carolina Conference Council on Ministries.

He is married to the former Marilyn Jane Morris of Chapel Hill, North Carolina.

A